Food for Life, Love, and Looks

DP The Danbury Press

WOMAN ALIVE

Food for Life, Love, and Looks

by Dilys Wells

Inter **i** bérica, S.A. de Ediciones

Series Coordinator: John Mason
Design Director: Guenther Radtke
Picture Editor: Roger Hyde
Editor: Judith Schecter
Copy Editor: Mitzi Bales
Research: Marian Pullen
Consultants: Beppie Harrison
              Jo Sandilands

Contents

Whether you are one of those who eats to live, who lives to eat, or who falls somewhere in the middle of the extremes, this book will offer much to you. Here are numerous food facts—some new, some old—that will help you look and feel your best. Among the helpful guidelines are how to buy food both for variety and nutritional balance; proper ways of food storage to retain food value and save money; and what you should know about health foods and fads. Diets are discussed in two important sections: one on reducing diets, which also includes adjusted diets for that often neglected group, the too thin; another on restricted diets for the ill. Now is the time—and this is the book to help you—to alter your approach to food. You will reap benefits in renewed energy and vitality for you and family.

Our Daily Bread

Every region of the world has a food that is most basic to the diet—the staple that sustains life for the most humble as well as the better off. Be it wheat in the form of bread, rice or other cereal grain, potatoes, or pasta, it is the most important food of life.

Below: wheat has been cultivated since the days of the earliest civilizations, and is one of the world's most important products.

Right: it was the struggle of Indian slaves on the Spanish plantations of Hispaniola that provided sugar for wealthy Europeans.

Above: African women today still dry and pound the grain they use daily in the ancient and timeless way of their ancestors.

Above: when Lord Sandwich called for meat between two slices of bread, he didn't know the snack would be known by his name.

Below: processed wheat flour paste becomes pasta—in numerous and imaginative shapes.

Above: millions of Asians depend on the all-important rice crop for their main food.

Below: seemingly endless mounds of earth are turned to harvest the vital potatoes.

Food and Ritual

Food has always played an honored role in the celebration, or observance, of important events: birth, marriage, religion, prosperity—even death. A table heaped to capacity is the symbol of the hospitality that binds people together in brotherhood.

Below: an Egyptian wall painting depicts the funeral table of food and drink laid to send a noble to a well-fed afterlife.

Above: rich Venetians of Renaissance days entertained sumptuously with banquets of many courses, as shown in this painting.

Below left: the first Thanksgiving. Pilgrims of New England feasted and prayed to celebrate the success of their harvest.

Above: Buddhist monks eat sparingly and austerely in strong self-denial that is an important part of their religious devotion.

Below: "The Health of the Bride" is toasted in Stanhope Forbes' touching painting of a Victorian working-class wedding breakfast.

Above: the traditional Passover Seder, recalling the Jews' escape from slavery in ancient times, is a joyful family affair.

Above: Harvest Festival time is celebrated in an English country church with arrangements of the seasonal foods and flowers.

Delicacies to Delight

Every culture has certain food items that are considered rare delicacies—although one culture's delicacies may be another's offal. It is usually to honored guests that the costliest and rarest foods are offered.

Right: oysters for breakfast—that was the height of luxury in prerevolutionary 18th-century France, as shown in this painting.

Below: a medieval duke loads his table with rich and expensive foodstuff for the courtly throng that attends him, and shares his food.

Below right: the ceremonial presentation of a boar's head was an important part of any great feast in ancient and medieval times.

Above right: if you are guest of honor of a Bedouin sheikh, be prepared to receive the eye of a sheep as a special delicacy.

Below: expensive, and increasingly rare, the best caviar is the salted roe of sturgeon.

Above: snails are considered a treat in the French cuisine—and many gourmets say their preparation is the test of a good chef.

11

Preserving it

We have come a long way in preserving food, but many of the old principles still apply. Natural or artificial methods of heating, freezing, and curing enable us to keep foods almost indefinitely for later use.

Below: with no way of keeping food for the animals, medieval farmers had to kill and salt their food animals at winter's start.

Above: a huge catch of sardines drying on special racks in the warm Portuguese sun.

Below: fascinated American schoolchildren of the late 1800's watch an iceman prepare a chunk of ice to go into someone's icebox.

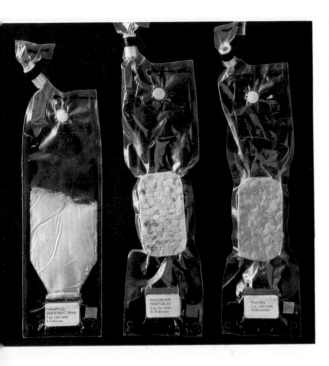

Above: modern freeze-dry methods provide astronauts with a complete meal in space.

Above right: in Europe, as here, convenient canned goods are available in big variety.

Below: it has to be just the right amount of drying to turn juicy grapes from the island of Crete into plump, sun-ripened raisins.

Below: well-stocked home freezers assure an unlimited selection of foods in all seasons.

Cooking it

Cooking is one of the few elements of good housekeeping that allows a broad scope for creativity. In the preparation of tasty and healthy meals, imagination and skill play a large part—and mitigate the routine.

Right: Mrs. Isabella Beeton pioneered in writing cookbooks. Every wise Victorian wife had her *Book of Household Management.*

Below: the medieval way of roasting meat on a spit over an open fire, with frequent basting, was a hot and time-consuming job.

Bottom: cooking was an all-day project in Colonial American times. Life centered around the warmth of the big open fireplace, which required a special method of cooking.

Above: pungent, sweet, strong, mild—spices give food distinctive flavor and tastiness.

Below: wrapping food in leaves and roasting it over hot coals was an early way of cooking. Hawaiians still cook this way for their luaus.

Right: modern ranges—even this British version that is smaller and different in arrangement than ours—makes cooking easier. But it's still the cook that counts most.

15

Good to Eat, Good for You

1

"We are what we eat" is a familiar saying. It doesn't mean that eating a pound of spinach will give you the strength of Popeye, or that eating a bushel of carrots will enable you to throw away your glasses. It does mean that a proper diet will put your body in the top condition required for replacing worn-out body tissues with vital new ones.

There is a regular turnover of body tissues. Ever wondered where last year's tan went? It has literally worn off, and has been replaced by new layers from beneath the skin. The same production of new layers applies when you break a nail, and it grows again.

You may think that your bones and teeth are hard, permanent structures. However, the calcium phosphate they are made from is constantly being removed into the blood, and replaced by fresh bone minerals. So the bones you have this year are not the same as last year's.

Scientists have worked out that the body completely repairs itself every seven years. If you are 28, then, you've had four complete body replacements in your lifetime. This constant turnover ensures that the body is kept as healthy and efficient as possible. Food supplies the energy the body needs to function in all its parts. For example, the muscle cells need energy to move the body around from place to place, just as the nerves require energy to see, hear, think, and smell. Lying in bed, fast asleep, we still use up energy.

There is nothing to equal the delight to the eye, and temptation to the tastebuds, as a mouth-watering array of fresh food. Our rich abundance of food in this country offers every family the opportunity of good health through good nutrition.

The heart continues to beat, and the muscles in the chest wall still rise and fall to inflate the lungs during breathing. Energy in the form of heat is needed for body warmth, and for maintaining a steady body temperature. An adequate, balanced diet will assure us that our bodies get all the energy necessary to keep in first-rate condition.

A balanced diet is based on nutrition, which tells us what and how much we need of certain basic nutriments. *Protein* is the main building and repair nutrient for cells. The most important foods supplying protein are meat, poultry, fish, cheese, milk, and eggs. About 25 per cent of the weight of hard cheeses, such as Cheddar, is protein. Meat, poultry, and fish contain between 20 per cent and 30 per cent by weight. Eggs have proportionately less protein—only 10 per cent by weight—while milk contains 3.5 per cent protein. The cereal foods—bread, breakfast cereals, rice, and pasta—also supply proteins. So do some vegetables, such as peas, beans, and nuts. Although foods derived from plants contain considerably less protein than foods derived from animals, they can still give us one-third of our total protein intake.

Certain important *minerals* contribute to the building and repair system. Calcium makes strong bones and teeth, and keeps them healthy. The best sources of calcium are milk, cheese, and wholewheat and enriched cereal products.

Red blood cells need iron to give them their color, as well as their ability to carry oxygen through the body. Apart from the variety meats—liver, kidney, heart—and certain shellfish, no food is especially rich in iron. We tend to pick up our iron in bits and pieces from different foods: meat, wholewheat or enriched cereal foods, vegetables, and eggs. Even potatoes contribute to our iron intake.

For good health, the diet must also supply about 20 different *vitamins*, although the body requires them in only tiny amounts. For example, the recommended daily amount of vitamin C for adults is 50 to 60 thousandths of one gram. Without this minute

Daily Calorie Needs

Active children must have enough calories daily to meet their demanding energy requirements. The three suggested meals have the right calorie value for three-year-olds, and go far to meeting calorie needs for children up to nine. Breakfast is solid : soft-boiled egg, sausages, whole wheat toast, and milk. Tuna salad, raw carrot strips, an ear of corn, tomato juice, and ice cream make a tasty lunch. Vegetable soup, grilled pork chop, peas, rhubarb, milk, and apple tempt dinner appetites.

Age Three

Three-year-olds—boys and girls—should have 1300 calories each day. They will get them if they eat these sample meals, or ones very similar to them.

Age Six

A six-year-old boy or girl needs 1600 calories a day. Add the additional 300 calories with such foods as cheese and crackers, cookies, or juice.

Age Nine

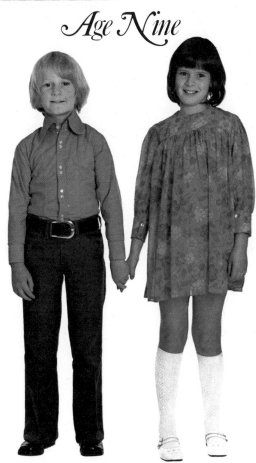

Boys and girls of nine years of age should have 1900 calories daily. Suggested additions: cereal, a sandwich snack, and potatoes with the dinner.

Above: meat is the main source of protein in our diet, and steak is one of the richest in this nutrient. For example, a five-ounce steak surpasses larger amounts of other foods in protein content, except for bacon and cheese. To equal the protein content of one five-ounce steak, it would take: 14 ounces of loin lamb chops, four ounces of bacon, nine ounces of pork chops (first row); 7½ ounces of boiled rice, five ounces of fish, six ounces of roast chicken, 10 ounces of plain spaghetti (second row); 12 ounces of wholemeal bread, 3½ ounces of Cheddar cheese, 32 fluid ounces of whole milk, 12½ ounces of soft white dinner rolls (third row).

but vital quantity, the health begins to suffer. Vitamin A makes for healthy eyes and a clear skin. We can usually get enough of this vitamin from green, orange, and yellow fruits and vegetables, including carrots, celery, apricots, and peaches. Certain oily foods, such as butter, margarine, and fat fish, also supply some of the necessary vitamin A.

It is believed that there are at least 13 different B vitamins, but they are normally grouped together into the B complex, or B group, vitamins. Most of them are needed to release energy from food in order to make it available for the body. Some of the B group

Below: large families with growing children can put any food budget to a tough test. Steak may be an easy and popular food for a crowd, but it's the most expensive. Also, steak doesn't stretch far—and is no healthier than—poultry, fish, cheese, eggs, or pasta dishes. Try cheaper beef cuts, and other high protein foods as main courses often.

vitamins are needed for blood building, and some to make healthy nerves. Most of the animal protein foods, plus wholewheat and enriched cereal foods, give us the required B group vitamins.

Vitamin C contributes to the connective tissue that knits together the body cells, but it is also important for healthy skin and blood. Citrus fruits, soft summer berries, and dark green leafy vegetables, such as broccoli and spinach, are the best sources of vitamin C.

Vitamin D works with calcium to make strong bone tissue. In addition to getting it in butter, margarine, eggs, and fat fish, such as tuna and salmon, we make our own vitamin D. When sunshine falls on the skin, the ultraviolet rays synthesize vitamin D. It is then absorbed into the blood stream, and used in exactly the same way as if it were taken in food. Adults can make all the vitamin D they need, provided they are not housebound. Children, teenagers, and pregnant women need more vitamin D than the average adult because they are laying down new bone tissue.

Two other vitamins, E and K, are essential. Vitamin E is found in small amounts in many foods, but the richest sources are vegetable oils, wheat germ, margarine, and eggs. It appears to be connected with fertility in some way, but its precise role in this connection has not yet been discovered. A shortage of the vitamin has never been recorded. It is likewise rare to be short of vitamin K, which is necessary to make the blood clot. It is found mostly in green vegetables.

The *carbohydrates* are used only for energy. They are found in sugar and sweet foods made from sugar, and in starchy foods, such as potatoes, bread, rice, and pasta. Carbohydrates are not considered essential, because you can be perfectly healthy without them.

Fats also give us energy. Besides butter, margarine, oils, and fat meat, there is fat hidden in cheese, milk, and eggs. Vitamins A, D, and E are found only in foods that contain fat. Certain constituents of fats, known as *essential fatty acids* must also be obtained for normal growth, and for a healthy skin.

Add water and roughage—mainly the indigestible cellulose from fruit, vegetables, and wholegrain cereal foods—and we have a complete breakdown of the food we need for a balanced diet.

Although all foods are made up of the nutrient substances so far described, different foods in the same food group contain different proportions of them. For instance, hard cheese is 25 per cent protein, 35 per cent fat, and 38 per cent water, while cream cheese is 4 per cent protein, 86 per cent fat, and 10 per cent water. Cottage cheese is 15 per cent protein, 4 per cent fat, and 70 per cent water.

Provided your diet has a balance and variety of proteins, minerals, and vitamins, the chances are that you will be eating enough of all the essential nutrients. You can live adequately on a low fat or a low carbohydrate diet, although it might be somewhat dull to some people.

We all need the same food constituents for growth, repair, and energy, but the actual amounts required vary from person to

Daily Calorie Needs

Adolescence brings the biggest spurt of growth. These three sample meals, which equal 2300 calories, can serve as a basis for the daily calorie needs of adolescents. For breakfast—orange juice, pancakes, bacon, and a glass of milk. For lunch—creole shrimp on a bed of rice, string beans, mixed salad, jello, and pineapple juice. For dinner—Waldorf salad, ham with pineapple, and cocoa.

Age Twelve

The 12-year-old boy or girl needs 2400 calories a day. The extra 100 calories can be added with a bowl of split pea soup, or something like it.

Age Fifteen   *Age Eighteen*

At age 15, a girl needs fewer calories than a boy. Her needs go to 2500 daily and his to 3000. Add them with bread, cereal, fruit, and cheese.

Being 18 and female means the beginning of watching the waistline, so 2300 calories are enough. An 18-year-old boy, however, needs 3400 calories.

Good health cannot be maintained by proper diet alone. Like all machines, our bodies require the right balance between exercising and resting its working parts to keep them at peak efficiency. See that each member of your family gets some form of daily exercise, and a restful six-to-eight hours sleep each night. By establishing good habits of rest and activity, you are helping your diet work best for your body.

person. Some people seem to absorb all the goodness from their food. Others don't use it as efficiently. So it is not at all easy to say specifically what you as an individual must eat.

If you are naturally slim, and find you don't put on weight easily, you can let your appetite guide you as to how much you need to eat. If you tend to put on weight easily, you can overstep your real energy needs without being aware of it.

That's some of the theory. Now let's look at a few specific food problems for you and your family. The energy value of a well-balanced diet for women will be too low for most men. The average sedentary man uses 2600 to 2800 calories per day. If your husband is more active, he'll require more calories, so let him have more carbohydrates than you allow yourself. However, too many rich desserts can make him a coronary candidate in 15 years. So try cheese and crackers with fruit for dessert as a change.

Although their diets are carefully chosen and adequate from every other nutritional angle, many women find they suffer from a mild deficiency of iron, which shows up as a low hemoglobin content in the blood. It has been estimated that one in 10 women suffer from iron deficiency anemia. Normally, iron is used over and over again in the body. When old blood cells are broken down, their iron is conserved for their replacement cells. But during menstruation, the iron in the blood is irretrievably lost, and must be replaced by iron from the diet.

This situation is aggravated by the fact that iron is one nutrient which is often diffi-

cult to absorb efficiently. Too much roughage, for example, can hamper the absorption. On the other hand, if you eat a fruit or vegetable high in vitamin C together with an iron-rich food, the iron can be extracted and absorbed more easily.

Children need proportionally more of all building nutrients than adults, which means that a higher proportion of their daily calories should come from protein. For the first 20 years of life, there are two main spurts of growth. The first is from birth until two years of age, by which time many children have grown to exactly one-half of their final adult height. The second is just before or during adolescence. Until they are ten years old, there is little difference in the growth rate of boys and girls. Then, girls begin their second growth spurt at about 11 years of age, reaching their final height by 16. Boys start their adolescent growth about 12 years of age, and continue until they are 18.

Stories of boys growing one foot or more in a single year are not uncommon. John is a 16-year-old dynamo of energy. He plays on the first-string football team, is on the swimming team, and runs in track. Like most teenagers, he has an enormous appetite. To cover his protein needs, he should have three or four cups of milk daily, a large wedge of cheese, two generous servings of meat, fish, or poultry, and a couple of eggs. These foods will also give him the calcium, iron, and most of the vitamins he needs for growth. Round out his diet with plenty of fresh fruit, salads, and vegetables—then fill in the corners with bread, potatoes, and pasta.

John is probably the only member of the family who can eat great quantities of starchy foods without putting on an ounce of surplus fat. But most of these starchy carbohydrate foods supplying energy are also sources of protein, minerals, and certain vitamins. Not so sugar carbohydrates. Sweet foods have a much lower nutritive value. In fact, many of them are simply carbohydrates and very little else. Between meals, then, John is better off with a piece of bread and cheese, or a peanut butter sandwich with a glass of milk,

Daily Calorie Needs

Because basal metabolism slows down with age, we need fewer calories daily, and we should eat less as we grow older. The three suggested meals total 1600 calories for a day. They are composed of: fresh grapefruit, omelet, and tea for breakfast; cream of celery soup, cottage cheese and tomatoes, and milk at lunch; melon, halibut steak, broccoli with hollandaise sauce, and tea at dinnertime.

Age Thirty

A 30-year-old man needs 2900 calories a day; he can add something to each meal. She needs 2100 calories, so can add bread, potatoes, dessert.

Age Fifty   *Age Seventy*

At age 50, a man needs 2600 calories; he can add bread, meat, potato extras. For her 1900 calories, the 50-year-old woman can add bread, dessert.

A man of 70 needs 2200 calories a day; he might add bread, ice cream, and potatoes to his menu; she needs only 1600 calories, as in the samples.

or a piece of fruit, rather than sweets.

The special nutritional requirements of a pregnant woman are geared to the growth of particular tissues, and the growth of the baby. To meet the extra demand for calcium, Catherine has doubled her normal intake of milk now that she is in her third month of pregnancy. She drinks three to four cups daily, and eats about two ounces of cheese. If she did not take extra calcium, this mineral would be withdrawn from her own tissues to supply the baby's needs. The same thing happens with other nutrients, too. Even though it may be detrimental to the mother's own health, nature makes sure the baby's needs are satisfied first.

To keep Catherine fit, therefore, her doctor prescribed iron tablets against anemia, and recommended that she eat an egg daily,

The draining effects of anemia can best be fought with an iron rich diet, which helps build up the red blood cells. However, the body will absorb iron more easily if foods containing iron are combined with foods containing vitamin C. That is the point to the two sample meals, which make the most of the iron they contain. Breakfast (right) combines the vitamin C of orange juice with the iron of eggs. The second meal complements the iron of liver with the vitamin C of a watercress salad.

plenty of meat, and liver or kidney at least once a week. Her obstetrician is keeping a close watch on how much weight Catherine gains, because overweight during pregnancy can lead to high blood pressure, and even toxemia.

As our food requirements increase at certain periods of our lifetime, our need for food usually decreases with age. This is because the rate at which the body works, referred to as metabolism, slows down. Generally, our energy requirements fall off from the mid-twenties. Therefore, if you eat as much, or even more, when you are 40 or 50 than when you were 20, you are bound to put on weight. Most women also tend to put on weight in middle age as they enter menopause.

The later years seem to be the most difficult time to maintain an adequate diet, especially

if you are alone. Margaret is a widow of 70. Her main problem with food is that she has lost interest in eating and cooking. Years ago, she used to enjoy cooking for her family, but now she finds little satisfaction in cooking for just herself. She eats only when she feels like it, and then, perhaps, it is only a cup of coffee and a piece of cake. Consequently, she is sickly and lacks energy. What can someone like Margaret do to improve her health?

Margaret likes soft foods, such as bread, mashed potatoes, eggs, and canned tuna fish, because they are easier to eat with her dentures, and take little preparation. These foods can easily be part of her diet, to which she should add fruit juice, leafy green vegetables, and some roughage—none taking long preparation. Rather than three large meals, snack meals every three to four hours would be better. Built on the foods she likes, but omitting unnourishing sweets as much as possible, these snacks will give her a better diet without changing her eating habits drastically.

One of the major problems of older people is the frequency of fractures, which occur as the bones become brittle in the aging process. A good diet can prevent this condition to some extent, especially if it has adequate calcium and vitamin D, the two main bone-building nutrients. Milk drinks, puddings, and creamed soups as part of daily snacks are easy and nutritious ways of getting the needed calcium.

Unlike Margaret, many older people tend to overeat. Calorie requirements are at their all-time low during the later years, while nutritional requirements remain high. If an older person eats easily chewed and digested sweet foods in preference to meats and vegetables, he will be overfed and undernourished.

The taste buds become less responsive as you age, so food should be well-flavored—but not too highly seasoned with very strong spices. To compensate for diminished taste, care should be taken to make the meal colorful, and eye-appealing. No matter what age, a feast for the eyes will make for the good appetites you want your family to have.

Bringing Home the Nutrients

2

Food shopping requires planning, patience, and a trained buying eye to spot a bargain that fits into your weekly budget, and planned meals. Careful shopping can save up to 15 per cent on your food budget. Over a lifetime, that could add up to as much as $12,000.

Next time you're in the supermarket, take a good look along the shelves and display counters. Look for foods that come straight from the farmer and grower to the store. The chances are that you will have to look long and hard to find any. Even among the fresh foods, you'll come across meat and fish that has been portioned and prepacked, and vegetables that have been washed, trimmed, and packaged. Fruit may be the only food on sale that has not been treated in some way by someone along its travels from the fruit farm.

By getting to know your local retail market, whether it is a small shop or a chain supermarket, you will get the most nutrition from your food dollar. Learn the days your grocer receives a regular supply of fruits and vegetables. Observe whether there is a fast turnover in the fresh produce. If you know there is a meat delivery around 10 a.m., it makes sense to shop in the late morning before lunch. That way you're sure to get fresher meat—and a bigger choice, too.

At the height of their season, some fruits and vegetables flood the market, and are offered at a low price to ensure a quick sale. This is a break for you, because fruit and vegetables at the height of their season are tops when it comes to nutritional value. Buy them at this time to enjoy them at their best and cheapest.

When you're looking for a bargain at the fruit and vegetable counter, remember that inexpensive spinach will give you far more food value — especially vitamin C — than asparagus, zucchini, and eggplant. For best sources of vitamin C, choose the citrus fruits— oranges, tangerines, grapefruit, limes, and lemons—and the soft berry fruits—straw-

berries, raspberries, cranberries, and blueberries.

Grapes, peaches, pears, apples, bananas, melons, and pineapples are delicious, but come much lower down the vitamin C scale. An average sized orange, or four ounces of fresh strawberries give you as much vitamin C as you would need for a whole day. To get all your day's vitamin C from apples, you would need to eat more than 2½ pounds. Plums and pears have so little vitamin C that you would need to eat four pounds of either of them for one day's supply.

Price is much affected by supply and demand. The most popular meats, for example, are those that are tender, and quick to prepare, such as steaks and chops. These cuts are the meat mainstays of many kitchens in which the less expensive, larger roasts appear only on a relaxed Sunday. Therefore, the butcher can ask a higher price for his steaks, chops, and other tender cuts because he knows they are always in demand.

Now take a look at the prices of fresh, frozen, and canned fish. Sole is far more expensive than haddock; canned salmon costs more than canned tuna. But cheap and expensive fish have similar nutritional value. Cheaper, coarse fish is just as good for you as fish in the top price bracket. The main difference is that you have to take more care in cooking the coarser fish to get it to taste as good as the prime fish. Try cooking it with fresh lemon juice and a simple fish stock for improved tenderness and taste.

Read the newspaper ads that usually appear at the end of the week to see what the stores in your area are offering. If they are foods you normally buy, take advantage of the offers, and stock up on these bargains. If the special offers are brands you haven't tried before, take a good look at the label. Check on the weight of the food in the can or package, and the number of servings you get from it. The ingredients are listed in the order of the amount of each contained, with the most first.

One unmistakable consumer fact in the 1970's is that every year we buy more and more convenience foods. The majority of us spend between one-quarter and one-third of our total food budget on convenience foods alone—and the range of convenience foods gets bigger and more attractive all the time.

However, practically everything we eat—although we may not class an item strictly

as a convenience food—passes through the hands of a food processor at some stage or other. His part may be a simple thing, such as washing and wrapping vegetables. On the other hand, the food may be completely prepared and cooked, ready for heating and serving, such as a TV dinner.

A fantastic amount of money is spent each year in dreaming up new products in the convenience foods range. Leading food manufacturers employ teams of research chemists, food technologists, chefs, and home economists to devise new foods to please us. Food packaging has developed into an art. Psychologists are consulted about the right design, color, picture, and wording to use on a package to make sure it appeals to the consumer. The actual choice of the packing material is extremely important, too. It must ensure that the food reaches the home in the condition in which it left the food factory— without any spoilage.

Some of the foods you see in the supermarket look so delicious that you may wonder whether it is worth spending the time and trouble making a dish yourself when the same thing is on the supermarket shelf, prepared for you. This will, of course, depend on you, on how much money you have to spend, and how much time you have to shop and cook. Whether our meals will consist entirely of convenience foods in 20 years will depend largely on the importance an individual attaches to food and family

Left: by preparing a few dishes in advance, and refrigerating them, you gain some free time for doing dishes that need last-minute preparations.

Right: if you store foods in the areas of your refrigerator as suggested in this diagram, they will stay fresh longer.

meals in the overall pattern of family life.

The great thing about convenience foods is, naturally, their convenience. You don't have to walk miles searching for special ingredients, nor spend hours in the kitchen. You simply open a can or package, and pop the contents into a cooking utensil.

A cupboard or refrigerator supplied with different types of convenience foods is like an extra pair of hands when you fix dinner. Each of us tends to stock up on the convenience foods we personally find most helpful, and which fit into our own individual style of cooking. Obviously, if you are a woman with a naturally light hand for pastry, or who finds it second nature to make a smooth, creamy sauce, then pastry mixes and packaged sauces are not for you. On the

other hand, you may like a little help with some types of cooking you find either tricky or time consuming.

In most homes you're likely to find canned soups that can also double as sauces; packets of dried herbs for seasoning; stock cubes, instant coffee, breakfast cereals; jars of sandwich and snack spreads; cake mixes and frozen rolls; and—when there's a tot in the house—cans and jars of prepared baby foods. The question is, if you eat a lot of convenience foods, can you still be sure that you are getting all the essential nutrients needed for health and good looks? Are prepared foods an adequate substitute for home cooking?

The case is not a clear-cut one. It it not a simple matter of convenience foods versus

Make the Most of Your Refrigerator

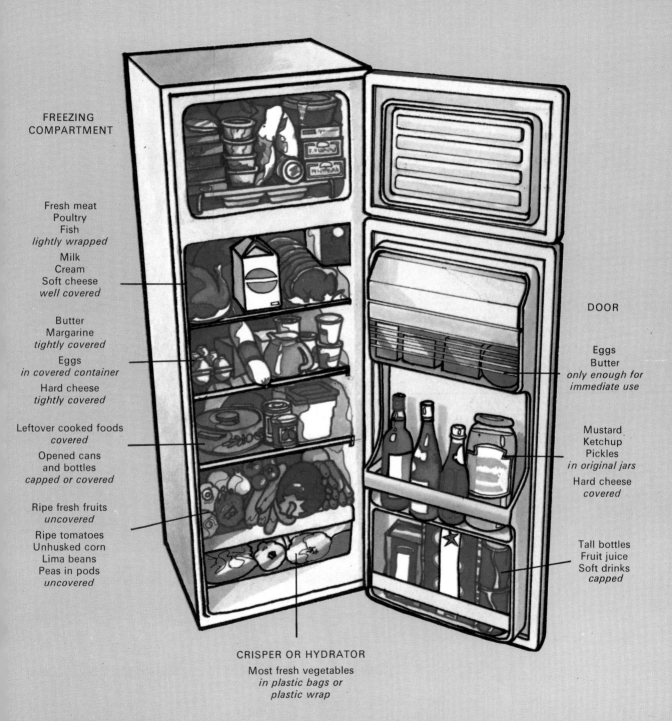

FREEZING COMPARTMENT

Fresh meat
Poultry
Fish
lightly wrapped

Milk
Cream
Soft cheese
well covered

Butter
Margarine
tightly covered

Eggs
in covered container

Hard cheese
tightly covered

Leftover cooked foods
covered

Opened cans
and bottles
capped or covered

Ripe fresh fruits
uncovered

Ripe tomatoes
Unhusked corn
Lima beans
Peas in pods
uncovered

DOOR

Eggs
Butter
*only enough for
immediate use*

Mustard
Ketchup
Pickles
in original jars

Hard cheese
covered

Tall bottles
Fruit juice
Soft drinks
capped

CRISPER OR HYDRATOR
Most fresh vegetables
*in plastic bags or
plastic wrap*

Your refrigerator is close to your most important household appliance. The temperatures will vary depending upon the size, construction, and efficiency of your unit; but generally, the air in your refrigerator is coldest in the compartment closest to the freezer. There is less variation in temperature in frost-free refrigerators. Take advantage of the variations by storing along these guidelines.

Know the Contents... Read the Label

In January 1973, the U.S. Food and Drug Administration revised the code for food labeling that gives the consumer all the necessary information about the food product he is purchasing. Here are some things to look out for:

NUTRITIONAL CONTENTS
Bread, flour, fortified milk, fruit juices, and other foods to which nutrients have been added, must list the caloric, protein, carbohydrate, and fat contents, plus the recommended daily allowance (RDA) percentages of vitamins, minerals, and proteins.

FAT CONTENTS
Manufacturers must give the amounts of polyunsaturated, saturated, and monounsaturated fats in their products.

If a product states the cholesterol content, it will be given in milligrams per serving and per 100 grams of food.

VITAMINS
Foods with less than 50 per cent of the RDA of a vitamin carry labels giving standard nutritional information.

If they contain up to 150 per cent of the RDA, they must measure up to the federal standards for dietary supplements.

Foods with an excess of 150 per cent of the RDA must be labeled and sold as drugs.

FLAVORINGS
Puddings that contain no artificial flavorings— for example, a plain vanilla pudding—would simply be labeled "vanilla pudding". If both natural and artificial flavorings are used, the product would be "vanilla-flavored pudding", even though the natural flavoring may predominate. Puddings that contain most or all artificial flavoring are labeled "artificially flavored vanilla pudding".

Carefully inspect labels of new food products to be exactly sure of what they contain. It wouldn't do any harm, either, to check the labels of foods you've been buying regularly. You may find that your usual brand of frankfurters are not made of all *beef*, as you supposed, but simply of all *meat*.

home cooked, fresh foods. Just as there are some brands of convenience foods that are more nutritious than others, there are also some women who cook to conserve the precious food value of their meals against others who cook most of the goodness out of their food. Take Carol, for example. She insists on giving her family only fresh products daily, and she honestly believes she is doing her best by them. However, Carol likes all her food well cooked. She likes meat that is crisp on the outside, and cooked all the way through with no trace of pink inside. This is what she calls well cooked, though others might point out that such meat is dry, with most of the nutrients lost in the lost juices.

Carol says vegetables must be well cooked, too. Partly because of this, and partly because she is fearful of being late with dinner, Carol either starts cooking vegetables over low heat an hour before dinnertime, or else she cooks them well ahead and reheats them for ten minutes before serving. Carol would be horrified if you suggested that she is depriving her family of valuable nutrients. Yet, she would do better by taking shortcuts once in a while, and using well-known brands of convenience foods, such as frozen or canned vegetables.

You should expect that if you buy good quality products from reliable manufacturers, most convenience foods will have the same food value as those you purchase fresh and cook at home. It is in the manufacturer's own interest to start with top quality ingredients, and to treat them carefully.

The main nutrients that are affected by food processing are vitamins, which can either be washed out of food, or destroyed by high temperatures. Vitamin C and certain B group vitamins are the major casualties. They dissipate when foods are washed, even before the processing begins. Further losses are caused by any preliminary cooking, such as blanching, which is an essential step before quick freezing vegetables.

For example, 25 per cent of the vitamin C

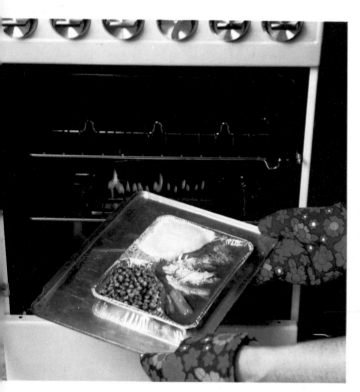

TV dinners solve the problem of a hot meal on too hectic days. Keep a supply on hand, ready to pop into the oven as an occasional fill-in.

in peas may be lost in blanching alone. The same vitamins are lost when foods are heated during canning or drying. Peas lose about one-third of their total vitamin C when they are freeze-dried—a drying process carried out at below freezing point—but they lose about one-half of their vitamin C when dried by the more conventional method known as rapid air drying, which involves higher temperatures.

Generally speaking, the higher the temperatures used in processing, and the longer the food must be held at these temperatures, the greater the vitamin loss will be. Canned fruit keeps more of its vitamin C because sterilization of fruit does not require heating for so long, or at such high temperatures,

as vegetables. Practically no vitamins are destroyed by the actual process of quick freezing, although a small amount will be lost if the foods are kept for long periods in low temperature storage.

Cornflakes, which are heated intensively during manufacture, lose practically all their vitamin B. (Most manufacturers add vitamins after heating, but there is some question about the effectiveness of this effort to replace lost vitamins). Bread made with enriched white or wholewheat flour loses less of its vitamin B1 because it is not subjected to the same high temperatures as cornflakes. But bread may lose up to one-third of its vitamin B1 if slices are toasted.

In general, the only nutritional losses we

his diet has been convenience foods.

Are you depriving your family if you economize by using margarine instead of butter? Not one bit. Provided you buy vitamin enriched margarine, its food value can be superior to the best butter. Margarines made exclusively from vegetable oils have the added benefit of containing unsaturated fatty acids, which some people claim will lower the blood cholesterol level, and help to avoid the coronary thrombosis problem.

Other vitamins are not changed much by food processing. Some loss of vitamin A occurs when vegetables are canned. There may also be a small loss of vitamin E, but again, a balanced diet provides more than enough vitamin E. Some minerals may be washed out of food when it is being prepared for canning or freezing. On the other hand, if the water used is hard water, some of the water minerals are transferred to the food, and its mineral content is increased. Proteins may be slightly changed if high temperatures are used in the food processing. This may occur, for example, if meat is overheated during the sterilization of canning. Such protein changes are not very important. Fats and carbohydrates are virtually unaffected by either canning, freezing, or drying processes.

Apart from the nutrients that are lost during the manufacture of convenience foods, many people are worried about the things that are added by the manufacturer. Substances such as chemical preservatives, antioxidants, emulsifiers, stabilizers, and flavor enhancers, as well as nutritional additives, are the subject of much debate. Why does the food manufacturer use all these chemicals, anyway?

Any fresh food will go bad if yeasts, molds, or bacteria attack it. For many years, chemical preservatives have been used regularly to improve the keeping qualities of food by holding these food spoilage organisms at bay. We take our freezer or refrigerator for granted, but how was food kept fresh before they were invented? Our great grandmothers

have to worry about are certain B group vitamins and vitamin C. But when you consider that fruit and vegetables are the main source of vitamin C in the diet, these losses can be important. If you eat no fresh fruit or vegetables, and no salads, but have only frozen, canned, and dried fruits and vegetables, you could suffer a deficiency of vitamin C. Although meat is an important source of vitamin, if you had only canned and frozen meat, you could become marginally short of vitamins in the B group, unless you ate plenty of protein foods and vegetables that are high sources of these vitamins. However, there is no evidence that anyone has ever suffered from a serious nutritional deficiency simply because most of

39

Upright freezers equipped with revolving wire
racks and door shelves make it easier to see
most of their contents at a glance. Models of
this type are available in various cubic foot
capacities to fit the needs of your own family.

relied on chemical preservatives, such as vinegar, salt, or sugar, to pickle, salt cure, or preserve foods. Today, other chemical preservatives are also used. Chlortetracycline is used as an antibiotic dip for fish and dressed poultry to prevent the growth of bacteria. Sorbic acid stops the molding of foods such as bread and cheese. Many preservatives help to extend the shelf life of the product—that is, they keep the food fresh from the time the storekeeper puts it on his shelves until the time you buy it. Careful control is kept on the chemical preservatives used. Each is rigorously tested for possible toxicity.

Antioxidants can prevent the discoloration of fruits, such as apples, peaches, pears, and apricots, when they are waiting to be processed as either quick-frozen or dried produce. Other antioxidants prevent foods with a high fat content from going rancid. The strong flavor that butter develops if it is left standing in the heat is caused by rancidity. Two chemical antioxidants often added to food are ascorbic acid and tocopherol. These substances are naturally occurring vitamin C and E, and as such, may boost the nutritive value of the food, as well as keeping it fresh in taste and appearance.

The texture of many convenience foods depends on the use of emulsifiers and stabilizers. These additives prevent the ingredients from separating. For example, separation might occur in mayonnaise, in which oils are mixed with water solutions. Stabilizers also make products smooth in texture, and help to thicken them. Whipped desserts, mousses, ice cream, and puddings depend on these additives for their pleasant texture.

Recently some nutritionists and psychologists have been doing research on our attitudes to food colors. They tinted familiar foods in unusual colors—red butter, blue bread, violet hard-boiled eggs, pink potato salad—and gave them to participants in an experiment. The experiment showed that, even though the subjects were extremely hungry when they were given such food,

Homemade strawberry shortcake of freshly picked June berries makes a splendid surprise dessert for a snowy December get-together. Berries freeze well in combination with sponge cake, but add the cream only after the cake is defrosted.

they did not eat nearly as much as they did when the foods were left their natural colors. We like to see food as we expect it to be, and we enjoy it less if it doesn't meet our expectations.

Because we like our food to look attractive and colorful, certain coloring agents may legally be used, although manufacturers are restricted in their use. Many years ago, before Federal laws limited food additives, many colors added to food were harmful to the health. Now each is tested for any possible health hazard, and is only approved for consumption when the authorities are reasonably sure about its safety. It is then described as being "generally recognized as safe", which is abbreviated by food technologists as GRAS. Coloring agents added to butter and margarine, for example, are carotene or annatto. Both of these substances are naturally occurring plant pigments, classified as GRAS.

Flavors as well as colors may suffer in some kinds of food processing. The more intensive the treatment, the greater the loss in flavor. To can meat, the product must be heated for much longer than is needed just to cook the food, because heating must be continued for as long as is necessary to kill all known bacteria and food poisoning agents.

Such extended cooking always causes flavor loss, so food processors are permitted to add extra flavoring substances, or flavor enhancers. There are over 300 different flavoring additives that are permissible. They include aromatic chemicals, essential oils and spices, and traditional seasonings, such as salt and acetic acid. Nutritional additives include iodine in table salt; minerals and vitamins in enriched white flour and breakfast cereals; and vitamins in milk and some brands of margarine. At present the enenrichment of basic foods is carried out voluntarily. Many nutritionists consider that a national program of enrichment is desirable, especially to help those people who,

even in a country so generally well-fed and affluent as the United States, continue to be undernourished.

Who is responsible for keeping a careful check on what goes into our food? That job falls to the Food and Drug Administration (FDA), which is an agency of the federal government. The FDA also sets down standards of how foods should be labeled to ensure that their packaging is not deceptive about their contents. A new and stricter FDA code will be fully in effect by 1975. Meantime, the FDA requires the label to state clearly what's inside the package; in what form the food is—whether whole, sliced, diced, or chopped; and what it contains in terms of servings of food—for example, four servings of half a cup each. The producer's name and business address must also be shown clearly.

Other Federal agents who safeguard our food are the inspectors of the Department of Agriculture. They keep a close watch on meat and poultry from the time these foods are still on the farm until they are offered for sale. The inspection policy covers meat products and processed meats, including ham and bacon, and also imported meat. Meat is stamped with an official stamp after it has been inspected. Condemned meat must either be destroyed, or used for purposes other than for food.

Left: it would take all these ingredients—some of which are hard to find —and long preparation to produce the plate of chop suey pictured. Out of a package, it took only 15 minutes before serving. This explains the success of convenience foods.

Right: all the necessary ingredients for chop suey are in one convenient package, ready just to be heated. The part that would have taken much work is in dehydrated form with preservatives added—meat, vegetables, spices, and fat (top left).

Additives

Food	Additive	Function
Fats		
Salad and cooking oils	tocopherol	prevents rancidity
Margarine	mineral salts, vitamins	nutritional fortification
	annatto, carotene	coloring
Butter	annatto, carotene	coloring
Bread and Cereal Products		
Bread, rolls	calcium lactate, calcium phosphate	activates yeast and conditions dough
	calcium propionate	inhibits mold
Baked goods	certified food color	coloring
Cake mixes	baking powder, baking soda	leavening
Breakfast cereals	butylated hydroxyanisole (BHA), butylated hydroxytoluene (BHT)	prevents rancidity
	mineral salts, vitamins	nutritional fortification
Produce		
Fruits for freezing	ascorbic acid	prevents darkening
Canned fruits and vegetables	propyl gallate, BHA	prevents rancidity
Dried fruit	sulphur dioxide	prevents darkening
Meats		
Salted meats	sodium chloride	preservative
Breaded fish sticks	chlortetracycline	preservative
Meat pies	BHA, BHT	prevents rancidity
Dairy		
Ice Cream	sodium alginate	texture
	lecithin	prevents separation
Evaporated milk	disodium orthophosphate	texture
Fortified milk	mineral salts, vitamins	nutritional fortification
Cheese wrappers	sorbic acid	inhibits mold
Cheese	acetic acid	enhances flavor
	disodium orthophosphate	texture
Miscellaneous		
Diet foods	saccharin	sweetener
Pickles	alum	texture
Iodized salt	mineral salts, vitamins	nutritional fortification
Soft drinks	certified food coloring	coloring
	saccharin	sweetener
Ketchup	acetic acid	enhances flavor
Potato chips	BHA, BHT	prevents rancidity
Whipped cream in pressurized cans	carbon dioxide	whipping agent
French dressing	pectin	thickening

Ground meat must contain no more than 30 per cent fat, and no extenders at all. If your butcher or supermarket is conforming to the law, then, you can feel that a meal of hamburgers is protein rich, not fatty and starchy.

Many people are justifiably concerned about the wide-scale use of pesticides. When certain catches of fish were found to contain DDT far in excess of the safety tolerance, a Commission on Pesticides was established. Its aim was to investigate the use of pesticides, and to report back to the FDA with its recommendations. The Commission recommended that DDT and DDD be gradually phased out over the following two years, and their use restricted to emergencies. The Commission's other recommendations were designed to protect us from health hazards that might spring from food, water, or air contaminated with residues of pesticides, or radioactivity.

Left: our food contains many additives meant to stabilize or improve them as to color, texture, or nutritional value. Over 1000 additives are used in a variety of foods, some for more than one purpose. This chart indicates what some of the additives are, what they do, and which common foods they are in.

Right: a giant ice cream sundae owes most of its color, flavor, and creamy smooth texture to additives in the sauces, ice cream, and the big dollop of whipped cream.

Better Cooking and Storing

3

Above: a home freezer is a help to a working wife, who can cook ahead and store meals, and can also bring much eating pleasure to anyone by providing out-of-season foods. However, it is usually only the large family that finds it an economy.

Left: a conveniently arranged kitchen, with plenty of open counter space and the proper utensils, is an incentive to creative cooking. It can even lead to a happy situation of husband-and-wife teamwork.

The important vitamin content in the food your family eats depends on a number of factors. To begin with, it depends on how fresh your "fresh" food was when you bought it. It also depends on how, and for how long, you kept it when you got the food home, how you prepared it, and how you cooked it.

The price you pay for food is no indication of its true food value. When you select meat, remember that an animal carcass yields more meat suitable for pot roasting and braising than for broiling and pan broiling. This puts a premium on steaks, chops, and tenderloins, and makes them more expensive.

A filet mignon or porterhouse steak may cost three times as much as a piece of chuck steak of the same weight, but the nutritional value of the cheap and the expensive cuts are virtually the same. The main difference is that the cheaper meats are the tougher ones. Generally speaking, the cheaper the meat, the tougher it will be, but longer and more careful cooking will compensate for it.

Filet mignon can just be whisked under a broiler for a few minutes. A pat of butter, salt, and freshly ground black pepper are all you need to enhance the flavor of the steak. Try broiling a piece of chuck steak for only a few minutes, and it will be more like eating the sole of your shoe than a juicy steak. However, if you brown chuck steak in a skillet, and then cook it slowly in beef stock (or water with a bouillon cube added), a bit of red wine, a handful of flavoring vegetables, a pinch of oregano, sage, or thyme, and some freshly chopped parsley, the finished dish will be tender and full of flavor.

Some kinds of variety meats have the highest nutritional value of all. Variety meats include all the edible parts of the animal's carcass that cannot be classified as flesh, such as liver, kidney, heart, brains, sweetbreads, tongue, and tripe. Of these, liver, kidney, and heart not only have the protein content of other kinds of meat, but also have extra B vitamins, some vitamin A, and iron. Dietitians usually recommend that you serve liver or kidney at least once a week.

Unfortunately, these meats are not always popular. If you or your family are not too keen on them, look for a new way of cooking them. One way of disguising them is in casserole dishes with wine, onions, and pepper. Finely chopped liver added to ground beef improves the flavor of spaghetti sauce. Beef, liver, and mushroom meatballs

are delicious, and so is liver, bacon, and onion flavored pâté. Finely chopped kidneys sauteed in butter add a great flavor to your favorite rice casserole dish or herb stuffing.

Often eggs and cheese are the best food bargains in the store. If you compare the food value and cost of a cheese omelet with a serving of roast beef, you will find that an omelet, made with two eggs and one ounce of cheese, contains the same protein, but costs only half as much as the beef. Try gnocchi or homemade pizza, cheese soufflé, or cheese cubes tossed with a mixed salad. Offer up poached eggs in a clear soup, or oven-baked eggs topping a dish of diced potatoes and onions—there are literally hundreds of good ways of serving eggs and cheese. Such dishes can be delicious in themselves—in no way an apologetic substitute for meat.

Above: with the proper cookware, you can use any cooking technique. Broiling meat on a rack is the most fat-free way of preparing it. Use a steamer to help keep the nutrients in vegetables. Fireproof glass pots are fine for quick boiling vegetables, and a heavy enameled pot just right for poaching of fruits.

Right: future chefs in class watch the demonstrator use a pastry bag to pipe finishing touches on fancy hors d'oeuvres.

Right: vegetables that
are cooked properly will
retain their vitamins.
The rule is: the short-
est cooking time in the
smallest amount of water.

Cooking vegetables doesn't mean brutally boiling
them to a limp damp mass for 20 minutes or longer.
Brussels sprouts, for example, will lose both
flavor and vitamins if they are drowned in water
in an uncovered saucepan, and cooked too long.

To keep the goodness in all green vegetables,
cook them in only a little water in a covered pot,
over low-to-medium heat, and for only five to
seven minutes. Vegetables already contain water,
and this is released during the cooking process.

A popular French method of cooking vegetables
is with a wire basket set inside a pot in a small
amount of water, which circulates freely around
the vegetables. After a few minutes, the food
can be lifted out in the basket, crisp and green.

Green vegetables cooked with the lid firmly on
the pan can sometimes have too strong a taste
for some people. To keep the heat in, and some
of the extra strong flavor out, put a few lettuce
leaves on top of the vegetables as they cook.

Don't Kill Your Vegetables

DON'T

Select bruised or blemished produce.

Buy fruits and vegetables in quantities because the vitamin C content will be lost even in 2-3 days.

Store fruit and vegetables in damp containers or coverings that will permit them to rot.

Allow too much air to circulate around leafy vegetables; this causes wilted leaves and loss of vitamin C.

Keep leafy vegetables at room temperature, or half the vitamins B and C will be lost in one day.

Put fruit in the refrigerator if it is not ripe; instead let it ripen slowly on a windowsill or counter, then refrigerate.

Cut away many of the dark outer leaves because they contain the largest concentration of vitamins and minerals.

Wash vegetables in tepid water—and don't soak them; a cold spray is best and quickest.

Peel vegetables if possible—well-scrubbed carrots cooked a few minutes in a little water with butter are sweeter and healthier.

Salt vegetables until ready to serve, because juices and flavor are drawn out by salt in the cooking water.

Cook in an uncovered pan that will expose vegetables to light and air, causing losses of vitamin C.

Cook in large quantities of water, since all fresh vegetables contain a large amount of water.

The rule is: *the shortest time in the smallest amount of water.*

When you serve meat, make it stretch further by serving the traditional accompaniments, such as stuffing, dumplings, egg noodles, or fritters. You get the best food value in proteins by combining an animal protein with protein derived from cereals or vegetables. Therefore, because they are made with bread, cereals, eggs, and milk, these traditional dishes also make their contribution to the nutritional value of the meal.

To retain as much vitamin C as possible, frozen vegetables are best taken straight from freezer storage, and plunged into boiling water. Complete frozen meals and main dishes should also be put straight from the freezer into a preheated oven. The larger cuts of meat, poultry, and most frozen fruits are best if allowed to defrost slowly at the bottom of the refrigerator. However, it is always wisest to follow the manufacturer's recommendation for a product. This applies to dried and canned foods as well as frozen and fresh foods.

Preparing the food can determine whether your meal is healthy as well as delicious. There are a few golden rules that help to safeguard precious nutrients when you prepare food. Remember that some vitamins, such as those in the B group and vitamin C, readily dissolve in water. So, when you wash food, you wash away some of the vitamins. With the exception of salt meat, which needs to be soaked overnight to remove excess brine, you should avoid soaking meat, or washing it under running water. It is usually enough to wipe the surface of meat, poultry and fish with a clean damp cloth, or with a fresh damp paper towel.

Take care not to leave vegetables standing in water. Those that are especially rich in vitamin C—such as cabbage, broccoli, brussels sprouts, cauliflower, and spinach—should be thoroughly, but quickly, washed in cold water. Don't cut the vegetables into pieces before washing. The more cut surfaces there are, the more easily the vitamin C will wash out. Green, snap, or wax beans,

That Extra Special Flavor

Herbs

BASIL The fresh and dried leaves are especially suited to most tomato dishes, seafood, meats, salads.

BAY LEAF A strong herb called the laurel leaf; adds its special flavor to soups, stews, and is a *bouquet garni* ingredient.

CARAWAY A small seed that enhances any cabbage, sauerkraut or beet dish; also cakes, breads, cheeses, and stews.

CHIVES The only member of the onion family considered a herb. Delicate flavor for eggs, salads, fish, sauces.

DILL Available fresh, or in weed or seed form. Use seeds with fish or chicken; the weed with sour cream dishes, salmon, eggs, pickles, tomatoes, potatoes.

MARJORAM A member of the mint family. The leaves are best in poultry stuffing, soups, meat pies, lamb, and vegetables.

OREGANO Sometimes given the confusing name of wild marjoram. A must in tomato, egg dishes; ground or whole in vegetables.

PARSLEY Sold fresh in curly-leaf and flat-leaf varieties (Italian). One of the *fines herbes* and *bouquet garni* ingredients.

ROSEMARY The crushed spiky leaves enhance any pork, lamb, green bean, or boiled potato dish, dumplings, and stuffings.

SAGE The lovely pungent aroma of the ground or rubbed leaves complement any stuffing, cheese, roast pork, or lamb dish.

SAVORY Available in summer or winter varieties. The whole or ground leaves are best in poultry stuffings, ground meat dishes, peas.

TARRAGON A necessary ingredient to any *Bernaise* sauce, the herb should be used with a delicate hand in eggs, veal, or fish dishes.

THYME Fresh in *bouquet garni*, or ground in poultry and meat stuffings, and clam chowder. This aromatic herb is quite strong.

Nutmeg   Turmeric   Cinnamon

Spices

Fresh garden herbs and pungent dried spices add a flavorful touch to any dish you prepare, if they are applied with a delicate hand.

ALLSPICE Unlike its name, it is not a blend of spices. Use berries in any marinade, pickling, soup, or ground in cakes, cookies, vegetables.

CARDAMOM The seed spices wines, pickles, fruit compotes, sauerbraten. Gives special flavor to coffee, curries; a popular spice in Danish cooking.

CINNAMON The pungent sticks are best in hot mulled pickling or syrups; sprinkle ground form over fruits, puddings, or use in baking.

CAYENNE The ground pods and seeds of red pepper, it makes a pungent addition to pasta, seafood, and Mexican dishes.

CURRY A powdered blend of 10-40 spices, usually with turmeric (giving its yellowish color), coriander, cloves, cumin, ginger, mustard. For any curry dish; try with eggs.

GINGER The root is an important ingredient in Oriental and Spanish dishes, pickles, marinades; ground, it is used in baking.

MACE The lacy covering of the nutmeg shell, its flavor is not as delicate as its sister spice; puddings, cakes, fish.

MUSTARD Two types—yellow or brown (called Oriental); whole seeds in pickles, relishes; powdered in roasts, seafood, salad dressings, cheese dishes.

NUTMEG Best to buy the whole seed and grate as needed; use ground in desserts, breads; adds special flavor to soufflés.

PAPRIKA Milder, bright red variety or the special pungent Hungarian type; for fish, meat, eggs, poultry, and naturally, goulash.

PEPPER Added to almost all foods, the black peppercorns (dried unripened berries) are used more than the white, which are the pale kernels from the ripened peppercorn.

SAFFRON The rarest, most costly spice, its crushed threads are used sparingly in rice dishes, stews, curries, and fish.

TURMERIC A sharp spice related to the ginger root. Golden in color, it is used to color mustard, and as an ingredient of curry powder.

Cayenne   *Mace*   *Mustard*

Above: after a good, thorough soaking in plenty of water, your vegetables might just as well be tossed in the garbage bin for all the good they will do you. Some vegetables, especially the home-grown ones, have a layer of dirt. Wash, but don't soak it off.

eggplant, corn, green peppers, okra, mushrooms, tomatoes, and zucchini need only be wiped with a damp cloth. You needn't take as great care with the root vegetables, because their vitamin C content is minimal in any case. Celery, beets, carrots, parsnips, potatoes, sweet potatoes or yams, squash, and turnips can be scrubbed with a soft brush, peeled thinly, and trimmed if necessary.

However you cook food, and however carefully you go about it, there will always be some loss in food value. To begin with, any nutrient that can dissolve in water will dissolve in cooking liquids during stewing, steaming, or boiling. Besides the vitamins already mentioned, certain minerals and flavoring constituents will dissolve into cooking liquids. You can make these losses good by using the cooking liquid in other ways. For example, you can improve the flavor of sauces and gravies by using water in which vegetables, meat, or poultry have been cooked. Of course, you would not want to use the salty water from some variety meats, nor the overpowering red liquid from red beets.

When you're cooking poultry, add extra flavoring with vegetables and herbs to transform that cooking liquid into an aromatic stock. Skim surplus fat from this stock, and add a powdered soup mix. The result will be a soup with a homemade flavor. You can also save the stock, keeping it covered tightly in the refrigerator, and use it in your next sauce or gravy.

Although some of the nutrients washed out of food can be conserved in ways like these, nutrients are often destroyed by heat. These losses can never be regained. It is those same elusive B vitamins and vitamin C, so easily washed out of food, that are also destroyed by overheating.

Cut down on these losses by taking care not to overcook. This applies most particularly to vegetables and meat. Most green vegetables are best cooked in a very small amount of rapidly boiling water for between five and seven minutes only. Cooked for longer than this, the vitamin C content falls off dramatically. For example, cabbage cooked for 15 minutes has only half the vitamin C you will find in cabbage cooked for seven minutes. If you were to cook cabbage for 25 minutes, or reheat previously cooked cabbage, the

54

Right: leafy vegetables should be washed fast under a light spray of cool water, preferably in a vegetable basket that permits the water to reach all the leaves. A basket with handles makes drying the leaves as easy as a flick of the hand. Remember, don't wash or dry all the vitamins away.

Right: fresh vegetables can lose up to half their vitamin C in one day in the refrigerator, so proper storage in your vegetable crisper is essential. The rule: don't crowd vegetables, and don't leave them to wilt for days at a time. Dampened paper towels put over vegetables, and renewed daily, will make adequate moisture without causing mold. Leafy vegetables last longer if not washed to store. Those with a protective skin can be just lightly scrubbed, or scraped.

SALADS

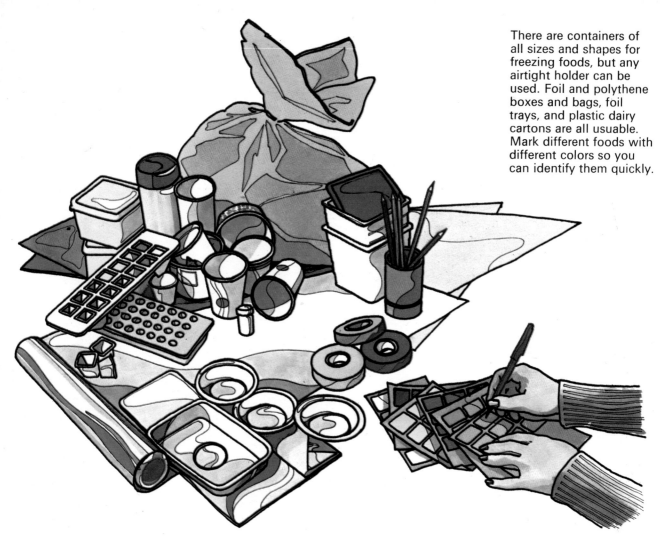

There are containers of all sizes and shapes for freezing foods, but any airtight holder can be used. Foil and polythene boxes and bags, foil trays, and plastic dairy cartons are all usuable. Mark different foods with different colors so you can identify them quickly.

vitamin C content would be virtually nonexistent.

Never add bicarbonate of soda (baking soda) to vegetables. True, it helps to keep their bright green color, but it instantly destroys any vitamin C they contain. Fresh or frozen green and snap beans and green peas have a little thiamine (vitamin B) that is destroyed if any soda is added to the cooking water. Cooking fruit is not such a problem as cooking vegetables, because the acid in the fruit protects the vitamin C. There are small losses, but they are usually as little as one-tenth of the total amount of vitamin C contained in the raw fruit.

As you cook meat, its fibers gradually shrink, squeezing out their natural juices. Any vitamins, minerals, and flavorings found in the juices then drip out of the meat. In roasting and broiling, the juices fall onto the hot pan, and some of the vitamins are destroyed by the intense heat. In moist cooking, such as pot roasting, braising or stewing, the juices help to enrich the gravy.

In no method of cooking should the meat be overcooked. The longer you cook meat, the more the fibers shrink, and the more juices are squeezed out. The result is that braised or stewed meat breaks up and becomes stringy, and broiled or roasted meat becomes hard and dry. In all cases, the meat has lost its good rich flavor, and a high proportion of its vitamins and minerals.

Meat cooked rare loses about one-quarter to one-third of its original weight, which gives you an idea of how much of the juices drip out during normal cooking. The losses are much higher when the meat is over-

cooked. Between 20 and 30 per cent of all the B vitamins are lost during normal cooking, and the percentage increases as cooking continues. Because the nutrients are transferred to the gravy served as part of the dish, stews, casseroles, and pot roasts usually retain more of their original nutritional value. The heat losses are also less because lower cooking temperatures are used. On the other hand, although high temperatures are used for broiling or pan broiling, the meat is cooked for a few minutes only. This short cooking time, in spite of higher temperature, helps to retain much of the original food value.

Starchy foods are unpalatable, and most are indigestible, when they are raw. By cooking, the starch grains absorb water, swell, burst, and gelatinize. Think of the difference between uncooked and cooked potatoes, or raw and baked cake batters. During baking, the starch on the outside caramelizes, giving the attractive golden brown color to baked potatoes, bread, and cakes.

When vegetables are cooked, their cellulose becomes softer, and the vegetable is easier to chew and digest. An average serving of raw cabbage in coleslaw would be between two and three ounces, but an average serving of cooked cabbage would be twice the amount. Although cooked cabbage does not contain as much vitamin C as the raw vegetable, you can manage to eat much more of it. In this way, there is a compensation for the loss of vitamin C during cooking.

Some fruits undergo some of the changes

Vegetable Storage

Refrigerator Storage	Freezer Preparation	Freezer Storage
ASPARAGUS 2 days in perforated plastic bag	Wash in cold water, cut into lengths just to fit container. Pack loosely, not in bunch; blanch 4 mins. Pack alternate layers of tips to stalks in plastic boxes.	8-12 months
BEETS up to 1 week, loosely wrapped, preferably in cool storage place	Small, tender beets; wash, trim, cook slowly in vinegar water in covered dish in oven; cool, skin, cut in strips; baby beets can be frozen whole. Pack in plastic boxes or bags.	5-6 months
CARROTS 3-5 days in vegetable crisper	Only young carrots; scrub, cut and trim ends, then wash; blanch 5 mins., freeze whole.	up to 1 year
CORN ON THE COB Use on day of purchase	Young yellow kernel variety best; husk before blanching about 8 mins. Wrap in foil and put in plastic bags, tied securely.	8-12 months
GREEN BEANS 1-2 days, loosely wrapped	Choose young tender beans, preferably home grown. Wash, trim ends; blanch 3 mins. Pack loosely in polythene bags, tie and freeze. When frozen, pack more compactly, and retie.	up to 1 year
MUSHROOMS 3-4 days on rack with damp paper towels lightly covering	Saute in butter or blanch 1 min. in hot oil. Drain on paper towels; set in bowl; stand bowl in ice water to cool contents. Carefully arrange in rigid plastic containers with waxed paper in between layers.	3-4 months
PEPPERS 3-4 days, unwrapped	Choose all green peppers, firm, with glossy skins; wipe with damp cloth dry, remove seeds, and slice in $\frac{1}{4}$-inch strips; pack in containers, separating layers as above. Seal, leaving headspace.	up to 1 year
TOMATOES Bottom shelf of refrigerator 2-4 days if not ripe. Best ripened on window sill	Underripe tomatoes skinned as for *peaches*. (See page 61). Slice if large, or halve if smaller size. Cherry tomatoes freeze whole. Pack in boxes or bags in small quantities, leaving headspace.	9-12 months

Left: if a vegetable is usually served cooked, it's a good chance it is suitable for freezing.

that take place during natural ripening when they are cooked. Their flesh softens, they become more digestible, and, if cooked with sugar, they absorb the sugar to become much sweeter.

If it is impossible to cook without losing food value, why do we bother to cook at all? Early in his development, man found that cooked food was more palatable than raw. Whether or not man hit upon cooking as the result of an accidental fire that burned down the pig sty, as legend has it, man has been cooking his food ever since he discovered fire. Nowadays cooking has developed into a great art. During cooking we can blend flavors and textures of different foods, and we can add extra flavorings with seasoning, herbs, and spices, to make food most appetizing and attractive.

Food storage is as important in the store as in the home. From the point of view of hygiene, food storage units, such as the refrigerator, freezer, pantry, and cupboard, need to be kept extremely clean to reduce infection from food spoilage organisms. The bacteria, yeasts, and molds that are always in the air, and cover every surface area, unavoidably come to rest on the food we eat. It is impossible to get rid of these organisms entirely, but we can slow down their growing action by keeping food under refrigeration, or stop it by deep freezing food. If perishable food is not stored properly, these food spoilage organisms get to work. Bacteria infected food may not appear bad at all. Think of the dramatic outbreaks of food poisoning that are reported from time to time. People would not have eaten the food responsible if it had tasted or smelled bad.

Warmth and sunlight cause most foods to stale quickly. Three-week old eggs kept in a refrigerator are fresher than eggs kept for 12 days at room temperature. Keeping food of high fat content at room temperature will give them that strong "off" flavor. The fats in cheese, butter, and foods such as cookies,

Freezing vegetables is easy, and, by selecting the young, tender ones, you will get the best results. Blanch vegetables by plunging into boiling water; bring to boil again for the recommended cooking time.

Cooling the vegetable is the next step. This must be done rapidly in running water, or in iced water, until the vegetable is cold right through.

The vegetable must next be thoroughly drained—first in a blanching basket or colander, and then on paper towels.

The packing method will vary with the vegetable (see the chart on opposite page). You'll have little or no waste if you pack foods in half-pounds, which usually is right for one meal.

Brussels sprouts are best frozen by the bag-and-box method. Line a rigid polythene container with a polythene bag, and fill with the sprouts. Seal with a tie twist, and freeze until solid, about eight hours or so.

Remove the bag from the container. It will have retained the square shape of the container, making it practical to stack in your freezer. Don't forget to label each pack with the date, contents, and amount.

will turn rancid unless kept in a cool storage place.

Correct storage is important not only for keeping food fresh and wholesome, but also to preserve its food value. You can see it if something has dried up or has gone stale. You can usually smell bad food. What you can't see or smell is how much its food value has been reduced. The main losses are likely to be of B vitamins and vitamin C.

You know how leafy vegetables or lettuce

Right: fruits will freeze best if they are picked when firm and ripe, and frozen within 24 hours.

wilt in a warm room. The loss of vitamin C proceeds at the same rate. You can freshen up leafy vegetables and salad greens by washing them rapidly in iced water, drying well, and popping them into the vegetable crisper of the refrigerator for an hour or so. But you can't put back the lost vitamin C.

The red liquid that comes out of meat,

Fruit can be frozen in several ways, four of which are illustrated here. In the open freezing method, fruit is arranged on trays, frozen until firm— about six hours—then packed in polythene bags.

You can cover fruit with a sugar syrup to freeze it. A 45 per cent (heavy) syrup takes 16 ounces sugar to one pint water; a 30 per cent (medium) syrup, eight ounces of sugar to one pint of water.

Fine granulated sugar can be sprinkled over fruit layer by layer, allowing about four ounces per pound. On thawing, the sugar will make its own syrup when combined with the natural fruit juices.

To prevent the discoloration that may occur in freezing some fruits, ascorbic acid is added to a cold syrup before it is poured over them. Drugstores have ascorbic acid in powder and tablets.

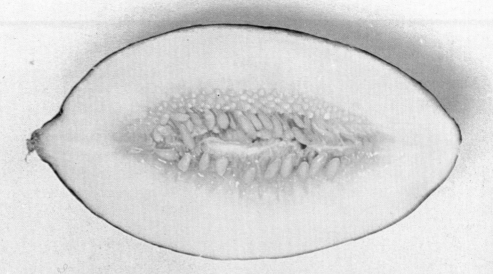

Fruit Storage

Refrigerator Storage	Freezer Preparation	Freezer Storage
APPLES 5-10 days lightly wrapped	Firm cooking apples, slice thinly; blanch 2 mins. Pack slices in covered polythene box, heavy foil between layers.	8-12 months
APRICOTS 3-7 days in covered container	Wipe, do not peel; prepare small quantities to avoid discoloration of cut flesh; stone, or freeze unbruised tender apricots whole in plastic boxes half filled with 30% syrup (8oz. sugar to 1pt. water); leave headspace.	without stones, up to 1 year; with stones, 6 months
BERRIES 2-3 days in covered container	Do not wash; choose firm small berries. Put 1-1½lb. in polythene bags, tie loosely; lay flat on wire baking trays in freezer 2 hrs; when fruit is firm, shake down berries, press out air, and tie securely.	up to 1 year
MELON 2-3 days when ripe	Cubes or balls; slightly underripe melon in 30% syrup with stem ginger for flavor.	up to 6 months
PEACHES 3-7 days in covered container	Blanch 6 seconds to remove skin; replace hot water with cold; slice directly into shallow plastic containers with 30% syrup. Crushed waxed paper under syrup surface prevents fruit from browning.	8-10 months
PEARS 5-10 days lightly wrapped	Choose small ripe tender pears; peel, core, quarter; cook 1½ mins. in wire basket in 30% syrup; drain; pack in polythene containers with cooled syrup poured over.	8-12 months
PLUMS 3-7 days in uncovered container	Select just ripe fruit; wipe skins; halve, discard stone; pack in 30% syrup in rigid plastic containers. Keep plums submerged with waxed paper method; leave headspace.	up to 1 year
RHUBARB 3-5 days lightly wrapped	Tender stalks cooked gently in 30% syrup. Cool thoroughly; pack in rigid plastic containers with headspace seal.	up to 1 year

even when stored in the refrigerator, contains vitamins and minerals. If you don't use the liquid in stock or an accompanying gravy, the nutrients are irretrievably lost. Unless you buy food for only one meal at a time, you must provide protected storage space for highly perishable foods, such as meat, fish, poultry, bacon, and milk; fairly perishable foods, such as butter, cheese, eggs, fruit, and vegetables; bread, cakes, and other bakery products; dry goods, such as sugar, flour, rice, oatmeal, packaged soups, sauces, and desserts; tea and coffee; frozen foods; and canned foods.

Generally speaking, for short-term storage, perishable goods should be kept in the coldest part of the refrigerator, that is, near or directly under the freezing unit. Salads and green vegetables retain their freshness in the crisper, and fresh fruit and tomatoes are all right on the bottom shelf. Most dry goods belong in airtight containers such as screw-top jars, or sealed plastic boxes. Remember to rotate according to purchase: that is, put the new milk behind the old containers on your refrigerator shelf.

It is best to keep bread in a clean, airy bread box. If you don't have a well-ventilated one, hang up a clean plastic carrier bag; it will keep bread fresh and free from mold. It is preferable not to keep bread in the refrigerator, because the low temperature causes it to go stale more quickly. Cakes, pastries, crackers, and cookies are best stored in airtight tins, boxes, or sealed plastic containers—but not together; keep moist cakes away from crisp cookies.

Your most economical storage unit is your freezer. Fresh vegetables can often be bought cheaply by the bag, rather than by the pound, and stored in the freezer. Buy only those vegetables that your family really enjoys, and that freeze well. Of course, there will be no saving at all if you are left with half a sack of eggplants, turnips, or carrots at the end of the season. But you can always share a bulk purchase with friends and neighbors.

Call on all members of the family to help with preparing, blanching, and packing the vegetables in suitable family-sized packs for freezing. Peaches, plums, strawberries, raspberries, cranberries, and blueberries are excellent to tuck away in your freezer for winter months. If you have a way of getting apples that have been blown from the tree by the wind, do so. Lightly poached or made into sauce, apples freeze extremely well. Apples also make a good partner for other fruits, especially strawberries, blackberries, and rhubarb.

Always freeze only top quality produce. No foods will improve with freezing, although second-grade fruit can be frozen well in puree form for later use in dessert sauces, ice cream, or fruit sherbet.

If you can afford the initial outlay, you

Two important things to remember about freezing meat: one, only freeze meat that has been hung for the right length of time, which your butcher can probably advise you on; two, quick freeze only small quantities at a time if you are not on a food buying plan. When it comes to thawing, remember that raw meat is best thawed overnight in the refrigerator. With slow thawing in its original package, meat will drip blood less, and so minimize the loss of valuable vitamin nutrients.

Fish & Meat Storage

	Refrigerator Storage	Freezer Preparation	Freezer Storage
FISH ★ fillet fish □ whole fish	Preferable to cook the same day; do not keep longer than 24 hrs. wrapped in waxed paper	*Must* be fresh. Foil between pieces in polythene bags or in ovenproof dish. Can be frozen with stuffing.	at 0° or lower 4 months ★ □
△ shellfish	cook and refrigerate shrimp if stored more than 24 hrs., crab, refrigerated up to 24 hrs., fresh scallops, live clams, and oysters at 32° for several days	Kept in prepackaged bags or boxes and deep-frozen as soon as possible. Do not allow chance for defrosting.	2-3 months △
● cooked fish	2 days in closed container	Freeze immediately after cooking. Must not stand at room temperature, or more than an hour in refrigerator, before freezing	1-2 months ●
MEAT ★ fresh beef □ ground beef △ fresh prok ● fresh veal, lamb	Fresh meat, loosely wrapped, 3-5 days near freezer section of refrigerator Moisture-proof store wrapping should be removed, and replaced with plastic wrap or bag	If not purchased in bulk from a wholesale frozen food outlet, have the cuts butchered at your market ready for freezing. Better to buy cuts freshly butchered to your specifications rather than prepackaged meats	6-12 months ★ 3-4 months □ 3-6 months △ 6-9 months ●
†cooked meat combinations (stews)	Cooled, covered and then refrigerated 1-3 days depending on sauce (less for cream sauce)	Boned meat takes up less room in freezer. Choose lean cuts; wrap chops 4 or 6 to a package. Foil wrap, then seal in polythene bags	3 months †
POULTRY ★ chicken, whole □ chicken, cut up △ turkey, duck, goose	Not more than 3 days loosely wrapped in coldest section of refrigerator. Store neck and giblets separately	Whole birds: overwrap store wrapping with polythene bag and seal. Freeze *unstuffed*. Pieces: remove from store wrapping and freeze immediately in polythene wrap	6-12 months ✶ 6 months □ 6 months △
● cooked poultry, fried † sliced with gravy		Place at bottom of chest or along walls of upright where temperature is lowest.	3 months ● 3-6 months †

Proper thawing of freezer-stored food will ensure it has the same flavor as the day it went into your freezer.
You may cook unthawed vegetables, cooked preparations
Slow refrigerator thawing is best for meats, fish, poultry
Thawing in cold running water is suitable for food wrapped in sealed packages or containers
Once food is thawed it must be used immediately to prevent deterioration of flavor

can save a good deal by buying meat in large quantities for deep freezing. The most economical way is usually to buy the entire carcass of an animal, or perhaps a half or quarter of a large one, such as a steer. Again, it will be no saving at all if you are left with pounds and pounds of the tougher, fatter, and bonier pieces that your family refuses to eat. If they love lamb stew made with the tougher pieces, or if you will trouble to make meat pâté with fat pork for those unexpected guests, or if you can do varied beef stews and ground meat dishes, go for the whole animal. If they insist on grills and roasts, you can still make a saving—but only a small one—by buying large quantities of the appropriate cuts.

During freezing there are small losses of vitamins B and C. There may also be some mineral losses if meat drips a lot while defrosting. To prevent this loss, make sure the meat is frozen as fast as possible, preferably against the freezer walls, and allow it to defrost slowly in the refrigerator. Never try to hurry up the defrosting of large cuts—the dripping will be so great that much of the minerals and vitamins will be lost. Thinner pieces of meat, such as steaks and chops, can be broiled or fried straight from the freezer.

It is important to wash vegetables quickly in cold water, trim them, cut them into suitable pieces, and blanch them for just the recommended time. Overcooking at this stage can cause excessive loss of vitamin C. The nutritional losses during freezing and storage at low temperature have little effect on food value. Prewashing and blanching are the processes that require special attention.

All foods for freezing must be carefully wrapped in plastic or foil to prevent the food from drying out. Select heavy-duty products that are strong enough to withstand the necessary low temperatures. Plastic boxes, waxed cartons, heavy-duty bags, and freezer foil must be used to keep the food fresh, and preserve its flavor. Food that is not properly wrapped dries out quickly. The moisture from the food itself usually causes most of the buildup of ice around the freezing unit. Also,

flavors pass from one food to another if the different foods are not well wrapped. So, remember that you may have salmon-flavored layer cakes if you don't wrap the strongly flavored salmon with an airtight covering.

Finally, keep a list of when you put each package into the freezer, and label each packet with the contents, quantity, and packing date. Don't keep food for longer than the recommended time. It will gradually lose flavor and food value if it is kept too long. Provided you use your freezer with care, and stock up with foods as they become cheap and plentiful, you can eat economically and well throughout the year.

There are some foods that just do not stand up to home deep freezing methods. It is better to check a home freezing book than to be disappointed.

Don't Try to Freeze...

salad vegetables, especially lettuce and cucumber

root vegetables, raw potatoes
unusable and limp when thawed

bananas
freeze to mush—don't include in mixed fruit or puddings

untreated melon
changes color and flavor

raw mushrooms
all right if sliced, sauteed, or blanched for 60 seconds, and drained

tomatoes for salad
only freeze sliced, and use instead of canned tomatoes

cured fish and meat
for longer than 2 weeks; salt content will turn ham, bacon, kippers rancid

light cream
will separate; however, heavy cream freezes well

mayonnaise
will thaw with taste and consistency of glue

sauces with egg yolks (Hollandaise and Bernaise)
will not recover the consistency with any amount of beating or cold water drops

chopped egg or other mayonnaise-blended sandwich filling
eggs turn to leather consistency, and mayonnaise separates

Rhubarb, raspberries, and currants can be frozen by the dry packing method. Fruit is packed in securely fastened polythene bags or containers without the addition of sugar. The process is so simple, even the children could do it on their own, turning a big job into a fun project.

Are Health Foods Healthier?

4

Health food restaurants are increasingly popular because of the new interest in food quality and wholesomeness. Many vegetarian main dishes, salads of all kinds, and cakes and pastry made with wholegrain flour are some specialties.

The whole health foods craze is beset with misnomers. Take the term "health food" itself. There is no scientifically based evidence to suggest that the so-called health foods are better for you than other foods, or that you will be healthier if you eat such foods in place of commercially prepared foods. You can argue that any food that keeps you in good health could be described as health food.

In that case, white bread with added synthetic vitamins; cereals, fruits, and vegetables grown on land fertilized with chemicals and kept free from disease and plant pests by chemical sprays; meat from animals injected with synthetic enzymes to make their flesh tender; and canned, frozen, and other convenience foods containing chemical additives, will keep you just as healthy as the "health foods" counterparts: bread made with wholegrain stoneground flour; cereals, fruits, and vegetables grown organically on land fertilized exclusively with decaying plant and animal remains; convenience foods, including the popular vegetable substitutes for meat dishes, without any chemical additives.

The words "chemical" and "organic" are also commonly misused. To say that you want to eat food that contains no chemicals is a contradiction in terms, because all foods are chemical substances. Proteins, for example, are made of chains of chemical substances known as amino acids. A simple sugar, such as glucose, has a chemical formula. What do you think of this list of awesome sounding chemicals? Thiamine, riboflavin, nicotinic acid, inositol, biotin, pantothenic acid, pyridoxine, cyanocabala-

It's not good to be fanatically serious about health food, but neither is it smart to joke about it. After all, the aim is better food.

mine. These may sound like a lethal mixture of chemicals to you, whereas, in fact they are simply the chemical names of some of the important B group vitamins. You need some of each of these every day in order to stay healthy.

Health food devotees often claim that their food is better because it is "organic". What they really mean is that it is grown on land enriched with fertilizers such as animal dung and garden compost. Almost all of our food is organic, simply because it is composed of organic chemicals. Health foods are also often described as "pure foods". Does this mean that foods bought at ordinary stores are impure? Not necessarily. On the other hand, some so-called pure foods, although they may not contain any added chemicals, contain naturally occurring poisonous substances.

Dr. Magnus Pyke, in an article in the British journal, *Nutrition and Food Science*, writes, "If Sir Walter Raleigh—if indeed it was he—came from America bringing with him potatoes, they would immediately have been prohibited by our Food and Drugs legislation. Potatoes contain about 90 parts per million of a toxic substance, solanine, of which 400 parts per million have been associated with frank outbreaks of poisoning." In the same article Dr. Pyke describes the naturally occurring toxins in many of our favorite foods.

For example, horseradish contains a poisonous substance that could make you very ill—if you ate enough horseradish, that is. Another poison called "andromedotoxin" may be found in the honey of bees that have fed on certain rhododendrons or azaleas; another naturally occurring poison is found in onions. The list of natural toxins in foods we eat and enjoy almost every day is a long one. The most succulent strawberries and raspberries carry a plant poison; both nutmeg and parsley contain a chemical which, if taken in large enough quantities, can produce a hallucinatory effect; even milk can poison some people who are extremely allergic to lactose, the milk sugar.

Fortunately, most people are able to cope with the potentially poisonous substances found in many so-called pure foods. But knowing these substances exist helps us to maintain a reasonable attitude toward all kinds of food. Too often we hear only the voice of the health food enthusiast decrying all foods grown, produced, and manufactured with the help of synthetic chemical substances, such as fertilizers, pesticides, and additives.

We need to keep a sense of proportion about food. All of us expect our food to be both nourishing and wholesome. Many people are justifiably anxious about the number of chemicals being used, not only by the food manufacturer, but also by the farmer. It is disquieting to learn that our food may contain any of up to 2000 different additives. It is distressing to think that agricultural chemicals may be upsetting the balance of nature. For these reasons, many people are turning to health foods.

Health foods include foods especially produced for the vegetarian, wholegrain

cereal foods, foods free from chemical additives, and foods grown on organic compost without the additional use of synthetic chemical fertilizers or pesticides. Although many people choose health foods for ethical reasons, many health food manufacturers are not so scrupulous. The magazine *Food Industry Futures* recently said that *sales* of health foods are about twice as great as the total amount of *production* of health foods grown without any chemical assistance at all. This means that many health foods are being produced with the help of added

You needn't be a health food advocate to try some of the interesting and tasty products in a health food store. For a starter, honey in-the-comb might appeal to you, or the nutty flavor of brown rice.

chemicals. It follows, then, that many food stores in the USA advertise "organically grown" foods, but sell normally produced foods in their place.

Other health foods may not be all that they seem. There are many brands of muesli, a popular health food breakfast cereal, claiming to be "prepared according to the formula of Dr. Bircher Benner". Some of these bear little resemblance to this early health food. When Dr. Bircher Benner originated his muesli in 1895, his product contained more fruit than cereal. Many mueslis today are a much higher proportion of cereal, have sugar or honey added, and contain skimmed milk powder. Although they are nourishing foods—and, in fact, have a higher nutritional value than most other breakfast cereals—they are wrong in being described as "original" muesli.

On the subject of breakfast foods, many people may be surprised to learn that we owe that popular breakfast food, cornflakes, to one of the earliest health food advocates, Dr. John Kellogg. Dr. Kellogg introduced cornflakes in 1898 as a food suitable for his followers, the strict and religious Seventh Day Adventists. They were marketed as "Elijah's manna" at the time. He claimed that the "physical purity" of his product would induce the "moral purity" of his followers. We are also indebted to Dr. Kellogg for peanut butter, which he created so that his patients with few teeth could still derive benefit from what he called this "noble nut". No doubt Dr. Kellogg would be delighted to find peanut butter holding its popular place with American children.

The National Nutritional Foods Association is pressing for strict standards for all health foods so that the bona fide ones can be clearly identified by the consumer. If such standards can be introduced and enforced, only then will the consumer be protected, and only then will she be getting what she thinks she is buying.

Although there is still no conclusive evidence that health foods have a higher nutritional value than comparable foods produced in the usual commercial manner, many people claim that organically grown foods have a better flavor. Fruits and vegetables for sale in supermarkets and chain stores have to be grown to a certain size and shape. Few shoppers will choose a prepacked pound of tomatoes of which one is enormous and the others small and oddly shaped. The storekeeper wants to buy a crate of lettuce or

cabbages of the same shape and size, so that he can sell them at the same price without marking each separately. If he were not so concerned about selling, and you about buying, a uniform product, you would be free to choose your produce primarily for its flavor. This does not mean, of course, that the health food stores sell only odd-shaped tomatoes, and the supermarket manager has

no regard for the flavor of those he sells. It is just that priorities are different. The supermarket may also give more priority to the keeping quality of foods, and huge chains are concerned with bigger crop yields because their volume buying helps them meet or beat their competitors' prices.

Judging by the rapid growth of the health food stores, and their increasing sales turn-

How many of the health foods pictured above have you tasted? Chances are, many of these vegetable proteins are probably now standard items on your kitchen shelf. Nuts, beans, peas, vegetable seeds and their oils, and wholegrain cereal products all come under the natural food umbrella. Raw sugar comes from natural unrefined sugars, and the varieties of honey are as numerous as the many flowers that produce their sweet nectar base.

over, customers are prepared to pay extra for food grown on organic farms. Because of the special precautions that have to be taken to grow foods without pesticides and preservatives, you can expect organic foods to cost more. Yields of some crops may be cut in half if no chemical fertilizers and pesticides are used, and shipping and storage costs will also be considerably higher because the foods lack preservatives.

Although it is impossible to give an accurate figure, some health foods may cost between 30 to 100 per cent more than their normal supermarket counterparts. To many people, such high prices would be prohibitive at the best of times, but are especially so in these days of extremely high food costs. Given the choice, most of us hesitate to pay the extra premium cost for organically grown health foods.

Perhaps it is just as well that we do not consume a higher percentage of organic health foods. If we did there is a likelihood that there simply would not be enough organic fertilizer to grow as much food as is needed. It was a shortage of organic fertilizers in the wheat belt of the US midwest and around the Sahara that led to the development of synthetic fertilizers. If we completely rejected these and other scientific aids to farming and food processing, food would become in short supply, and food prices would soar still higher. The majority of people want a full supply of good food at a reasonable price, and it seems that growing food with chemical assistance is the way to get it.

Many foods sold in health food stores are what is described as *wholegrain*, which means that no part of the cereal has been taken away during processing. The main wholegrain products are flour, meal, bread, crackers, and cereals. Wholegrain products are often described as *stoneground* too. This means that the cereal is milled in the old-fashioned way, between heavy stone millstones, instead of the modern way, by steel rollers.

When the white flour is made, the outer husk of the wheat, known as the bran, and the inner wheatgerm are removed. Only the white inside of the grain, called the starchy endosperm, is ground. The inside of the grain contains anything from six to 18 per cent protein, as well as starch and certain minerals and vitamins. The main source of the wheat minerals and vitamins are, however, the bran and wheatgerm. When these are removed, the miller is taking away a high proportion of valuable nutrients. Most of the flour now has B vitamins and iron added after the grinding in amounts that are supposed to bring the content of these nutrients up to the level found in wholemeal flour. About 85 per cent of all white flour sold in the USA is so made.

In making wholegrain or wholewheat flour, the entire wheat seed with bran, wheatgerm, and starchy endosperm is ground into flour. This is made into bread that may be described as wholewheat, entire-wheat, or graham. Sometimes a little of the very rough husk is removed, and then the flour is described as wheatmeal or wheaten. It is made into bread often called cracked wheat, wheaten, or simply wheat.

The main nutritional advantage of wholegrain cereal foods is that they provide more roughage than their refined counterparts. Because refined cereal products are more popular with the general public—wholewheat bread, for example, accounts for only a small proportion of bread sold in America today—the modern diet tends to be short of roughage. Medical opinion remains divided, but some eminent physicians claim that intestinal disease can be caused, or at least aggravated, by a shortage of roughage. Here, then, is a positive advantage of eating wholegrain cereal foods. However, the benefit is equal if the wholemeal bread was made from wheat grown on chemically fertilized soil, as from organically grown wheat.

Many health food stores sell nutritional supplements, such as vitamin pills and tonics, for which the manufacturers often make exaggerated claims. Vitamin E tablets are a good example. Their producers often

Kellogg's cornflakes were originally developed as a health food, and their inventor, Dr. Kellogg, also created peanut butter for health purposes. Today, these two foods are fixtures on every grocery store shelf, their popularity assured by children who prefer them to almost all other foods.

73

We may not be able to always eat right. Often, pressures of time, or of work, force us to skip a meal, or make do with a few cups of coffee. Even the best-intentioned diet can go haywire occasionally. For some people, a supplementary vitamin pill is the temporary answer. If you usually eat a balanced diet, you don't need a multivitamin pill, but you may be lacking in one particular vitamin. Shown here are the food groups necessary for good daily nutrition, and the vitamin supplements that are somewhat equivalent. If you skip out on some of these natural foods, you may want to take a vitamin pill instead. But, remember that eating the food in its natural state is healthier and tastier.

1. meat and eggs: iron; 2. grain cereals and whole wheat: vitamin E; 3. seafoods: kelp; 4. kidney and dairy products: vitamin B complex; 5. yogurt, cheese, and milk: calcium; 6. vegetables, offal, and dairy products: vitamin A; 7. green vegetables and citrus fruit: vitamin C.

claim that vitamin E pills will slow down aging, increase athletic performance and potency, improve a woman's appearance in a variety of ways, and make her more fertile. Most of these claims are unsubstantiated. No human being has ever been found to be suffering from a shortage of vitamin E, because it is so widely distributed in many of the foods we eat regularly.

Public imagination was obviously captured when scientists nicknamed vitamin E the "fertility" or "youth" vitamin. To date, however, rats previously kept on a diet deficient in vitamin E are the only creatures that show dramatic benefits with vitamin E supplements. From time to time, doctors will prescribe vitamin E tablets to women who have miscarried many times. While there is still doubt about whether it helps in human fertility—but as no danger is attached to taking extra vitamin E—it is thought to be worth a try.

Another current fashion is to have regular injections of vitamin B12. Many people claim that they feel wonderfully well after this vitamin shot, but unless they had been

74

suffering from pernicious anemia in the first place, the benefit of the injection will probably have been a psychological one.

Do enormous doses of vitamin C help to keep you free of colds? When an eminent scientist like Linus Pauling tells us it does, other scientists have to treat his theory with respect. Surveys and experiments are being conducted to find out whether massive doses of vitamin C—the equivalent of eating more than 40 oranges a day—really guard against colds, or help to cure a cold once caught. The results are still not conclusive. Some

volunteers given dummy tablets of sugar, or a similar inactive substance, appeared to do as well as those taking vitamin C to fight the cold bug. Again, you can't discount the psychological effect. Chances are that if you take a tablet expecting it to do you good, it will; but the reverse is also true.

Other vitamins frequently taken in the hope that they will guard against colds and other infections are vitamins A and D. If your diet is well varied, and you have enough to eat, there is little chance that you will run a risk of a shortage of these two vitamins.

Children, however—especially babies and tots—often need extra vitamin A and D. These should be prescribed by your doctor, and not just used on your own, because children can get too much of these vitamins. Some years ago, when some children were suffering from mysterious complaints, it was found that the cause was an excessive intake of either vitamin A or vitamin D. So it is wise to be guided by your doctor.

Other products often sold in health food stores are "elixirs" or "tonics" that are supposed to make you feel like a new woman. On analysis, many of these products are, indeed, found to contain a variety of nutrients, but usually in only a small proportion of the required daily amount. Many of this type of product are expensive, and you would do better to spend your money on more meat, eggs, cheese, and fresh fruit. You will derive more nutritional benefit from the foods—and certainly much more pleasure from eating them.

If you feel run down, tired, listless, nervous, or depressed, you should consult your doctor before trying nutritional supplements as the cure. The doctor should be able to advise you if you are marginally short of any nutrients. Remember that the only deficiency women are likely to suffer from is a shortage of iron, so iron tablets are the only nutritional supplement you will probably need.

Many health food stores started in business by supplying special natural foods for vegetarians, a group that still accounts for steady health food sales. The *ovolacto vegetarian* diet

Left: nut rolls, a long-time favorite with vegetarians because of their high protein content and tastiness, might appeal to your family as a main dish other than meat.

Right: fresh fruit and vegetables, especially in their raw state, form the basis of the vegetarian diet. Critics of this kind of restricted diet point out that it lacks the proteins and vitamin B_{12} that we get from meat. But vegetarians who include eggs, cereal, and dairy foods daily are probably getting adequate protein.

is similar to the usual diet except that meat, poultry, and fish are excluded. No animal fats are allowed either, but eggs, milk, and cheese may be eaten in unlimited amounts for needed protein.

The basis of vegetarian belief is that no animal should be killed to provide human food. That famous vegetarian George Bernard Shaw said that when he died, his hearse should be followed not by mourners in coaches, but by herds of oxen, sheep, and swine, flocks of poultry, and a small traveling aquarium of live fish—all wearing white scarves in honor of the man who perished rather than eat his fellow creatures.

Nutritionally, eggs, cheese, and milk are perfect substitutes for meat, poultry, and fish, but vegetarian meals have to be prepared with imagination to avoid monotony. Finding interesting new dishes that suit the

housekeeping budget, as well as the vegetarian's own taste in food, can be a test for the imagination. Vegetable pies, nut cutlets and croquettes, vegetables au gratin, vegetable curries, stuffed sweet peppers, eggplant and zucchini casseroles, cheese strudels, and gnocchi—these are some of the most delicious of vegetarian fare. However, most are time-consuming to prepare, which explains the success story of convenience foods for the vegetarian.

The stricter vegetarians will eat absolutely nothing that has been derived from animals. This not only cuts out eggs, cheese, and milk, but also butter, some margarines, cream, yogurt, and most prepared and processed foods that may contain small amounts of animal fats. People following this restricted diet are called *vegans*.

Normally, about two-thirds of our protein,

and a majority of our vitamins are derived from animal products. The vegan must have a very hearty appetite—and also a robust digestive system—to derive the same protein and vitamin value from vegetable and cereal foods alone. For example, to get as much protein as you would get from one average egg, you would need to eat nine ounces of boiled rice; or six ounces of boiled spaghetti; or three ounces of boiled lentils; or two ounces of walnuts. Eating all these quantities of rice, spaghetti, lentils, and walnuts would still give you less than half the protein you need for one day.

Although it is possible to choose a diet with enough protein exclusively from plant sources, there is still one vital nutrient that would be missing. Vitamin B12, which is needed for the correct building of blood cells, and without which you may develop perni-cious anemia, is found only in animal foods. Vegans are usually allowed to take special tablets of vitamin B12. Occasionally, cases of vitamin B12 deficiencies are reported among vegans, especially in families that have kept strictly to a vegan diet for several generations.

Recently the Zen macrobiotic diet has become popular, especially among young people. This diet is supposed to ensure rejuvenation, longevity, and spiritual rebirth. Anyone who follows the diet strictly is sup-posed to be guaranteed freedom from all diseases, and even serious complaints, such as diabetes, are said to disappear by con-scientious adherence to the diet.

It should be stressed immediately that there is no hope that such promises will be fulfilled unconditionally. In fact, the diet has been severely condemned by several medical authorities. The Council on Foods and Nutrition of the American Medical Association has described the Zen macrobiotic diet as "one of the most dangerous dietary regimens, posing not only serious hazards to the health of the individual, but even to life itself."

The macrobiotic diet is based almost exclusively on wholegrain cereal foods. Followers begin by reducing their intake of animal foods, fruit, and vegetables, and by eating more unrefined cereal foods in their place. Eventually, they are supposed to eat only cereals, with a few selected vegetable seeds and vegetables being permitted occasionally. Fluid intake is also severely restricted, which is one of the most serious aspects of the diet, and cases of kidney disease or impaired kidney function have been reported.

At all stages in the macrobiotic diet, the dieter must observe the correct balance between *yin* and *yang* foods. These rules are based on ancient Oriental principles, but no scientific principles have been discovered for maintaining such a balance. Yin foods are supposed to be the passive female ones, while yang foods are the active male ones. Scientists have shown that the so-called yin foods have more potassium than sodium, while the yang foods have more sodium than potassium. The ideal balance is supposed to be five parts of yin (potassium) to one part yang (sodium). Macrobiotic devotees claim that brown rice is the perfect food, because it maintains this perfect ratio. In fact, brown rice has a 20-to-1 potassium-to-sodium ratio, an inconsistency in the dietetic principles. Because the diet is so limited, it would not encourage overeating, which is certainly a point in its favor. However, anyone who keeps strictly to the macrobiotic principles may run the risk of serious mineral and vitamin deficiency, as well as a marginal shortage of protein.

The wise cook will find that the health food store sells many good things to help make our everyday food varied and interesting. Yogurt in all its varieties makes a delicious, inexpensive, and healthy part of lunch or breakfast. In the range of dried peas and beans, the health food dealers are likely to sell more interesting varieties than the ordinary store. Add a handful of these

Left: eggs are a good protein source for the vegetarian diet. A two-ounce egg is equal in protein value to: one ounce navy beans; one ounce cheese; 2 ounces walnuts; $3\frac{3}{4}$ ounces raw polished rice; $7\frac{1}{2}$ ounces milk; two ounces spaghetti; three ounces of wholemeal bread; $\frac{3}{4}$ ounce peanuts; $1\frac{1}{2}$ ounces cottage cheese; $1\frac{1}{4}$ ounces almonds; one ounce red lentils; one ounce split peas; $6\frac{3}{4}$ ounces yogurt.

Right: the Macrobiotic diet goal is the harmonious balance between the complementary opposites of *yin* and *yang,* represented here by white haricot and red beans.

presoaked dried vegetables to soups, stews, and casseroles for extra flavor, and as a meat stretcher that also boosts the nutritional value of each serving. Keep an eye out for large bags of dried fruits. They make delicious compotes, and spark a poultry or pork stuffing. Soak the mixed fruits overnight, and then lightly stew them, or keep the varieties separate if you prefer. Add a peeled orange slice, or a few spoonsful of lemon juice, for that extra tang. For children with a sweet tooth, dried fruits make a healthy snack straight from the package.

At health food stores, too, you have a better selection of wholegrain crackers and breads, which are especially tasty and satisfying with cheese. Also try some of the organic fruit and vegetables to test for yourself whether the flavor is better than chemically grown ones. Some of the vegetarian foods, such as nut cutlets, soya bean patties, vegetable fricassees, and meatless sausages, are also fun to try for a new taste. Soon you may find that, despite some increase in price, health foods will be a welcome and different addition to your meals.

Dieting for Looks
5

A good meal enjoyed among friends, or a pleasant evening at a favorite restaurant are among the most popular ways of relaxing. In fact, for Americans, they may be too popular. Enjoying a dinner with plenty of good food and drink a few times a week can contribute to those flesh pads at the waistline, and an extra inch around the hips. The reason is quite simple: if the energy value of your diet is too high, the surplus is usually converted into fat and stored around the body in fatty or adipose tissue, the long-term effect being a gain in weight.

There are some lucky people—usually young and active ones—who simply burn off any excess food. They can eat a great deal regularly, and never put on an ounce. Unfortunately, most of us don't have this convenient compensatory mechanism. For the majority of us, the long-term effect of regular overeating is an increase in weight.

Consider two different women, each of the same height. If you were able to weigh different parts of them separately—their bones, their flesh, internal organs, blood, skin—you would find that the different parts from the two women weighed very nearly the same, give or take a few pounds. But the amount of fat each woman carries could vary enormously. A slim woman of 5 feet 5 inches may weigh 128 pounds. Only about 20 pounds of this would be fat. A fat woman of exactly the same height may weigh 228 pounds—100 pounds more. She's carrying

Do you need to pare down a few inches around the midriff? To find out, take a long, hard, and honest look at yourself in a full-length mirror. Try to see yourself objectively, as others see you, from both the front and the back views—then make a decision.

120 pounds of fat. In extreme cases, it has been shown that obese patients admitted to a hospital have had more than 200 pounds of adipose tissue.

Some people attribute their more-than-average weight to being big boned. You can expect a big-boned person to weigh more than a small-boned person of the same height. But the body framework makes surprisingly little difference—only about ten pounds. The size of your hands and feet are usually a good guide to your skeletal type. A slim woman of 5 feet 5 inches who takes a size 8 shoe can expect to weigh about 10 pounds more than an equally slim woman who is exactly the same height and takes a $6\frac{1}{2}$ shoe. But when we talk of overweight, we are referring to an excessive buildup of fatty tissue, not bones, or muscle.

Of course, you need a certain amount of body fat. It helps keep you warm, acts as cushioning for internal organs, and gives pleasing body curves. If you have too little fat beneath your skin—the average woman, incidentally, has a thicker layer than the average man—you tend to look rather bony or scraggy. Thin people have their own problems with hollow cheeks, bony knees, and thin arms and legs. Very thin people also feel the cold easily. If you have too much fat, you begin to look—and feel—like an overstuffed cushion. The ideal amount of body fat is enough, but not too much.

People who put on weight easily don't necessarily eat more than those who can eat what they like and never put on an ounce. Often fat people eat far less than thin people. But if you put on weight, you are eating more than you need. Without complicated medical

Early in life we learn to compare our own size, weight, and figure shape with that of other people. You can't do anything about your basic bone structure, but it helps to know where your weight problem areas are, and how good posture helps.

tests it is almost impossible to say how many calories any one person should eat each day. Nutritionists have been able to show that some people need twice as much food as others do, even though they may be the same age, size, and sex, and lead equally active lives.

If you are reasonably slim and active, your appetite is usually a reliable guide to the amount of food you need to eat each day. Sometimes you may not feel like eating very much; the next day you'll take second helpings. This shows that the appetite is doing its work in controlling your food intake over the week. If you eat as much as you want to, and your weight stays at a steady level—within a few pounds over the month— the amount you are eating gives you all the energy you need.

You need to find how much you can eat to keep a steady weight. To do this, you may have to count calories as a guide until you learn how to use—or control—your natural appetite. It would be wonderful if the more energy you ate in the form of food, the more active and dynamic you became. But because the surplus energy is converted into fatty tissue, the extra weight tends to slow you up, instead of making you more energetic.

It's really a question of energy balance. The energy value of the food you eat is balanced by the energy you use in physical activity, plus the energy value of the fat that has just gone into storage. To lose weight, you have to tip the balance in the opposite direction. You have to cut down on the amount you eat so that the energy value of your food intake is less than the energy you use up in activity. In this case, the balance is made up by using some of the stored fat in place of food eaten in the usual way. Then there is a new balance between energy used up in activity, and the energy from a smaller amount of food, plus the energy from stored fat.

In simplest terms, the only way to lose weight is by eating less, and so using up stored fat. Every year there are hundreds and hundreds of diets published to help you lose weight. Many are faddish. But to feel well and look your best, you need a diet that is well-balanced. Even though you are trying to lose weight, your body still needs the same amount of proteins, minerals, and vitamins. Only the energy value of the diet needs to be adjusted. You must continue to eat the foods that supply the essential nutrients, and cut down on the sweet foods that are high in calories, but low in nutritional value.

We have said before that if you eat enough of the right kinds of foods to meet your protein requirements, you will also get most of the essential minerals and vitamins from the same foods. If in one day you had, say, an egg at breakfast, cottage cheese for lunch, a medium sized steak for dinner, and half a pint of milk throughout the day, you would certainly be getting all the protein you need. Add two or three helpings of fresh fruit, some salads, and two helpings of low-calorie vegetables, and you would have the minerals and vitamins you need.

The calorie value of this suggested menu? Just under 1000. You can add one thin slice of bread with a smear of butter to take you up to 1000 calories a day. If you ate only that, and were as active as usual, you would probably use up the amount of your own

What Shape are You In?

All figures depend on the bone structure underneath. Your basic bone structure is . . .				
	Pelvis slightly larger than average. Rib cage a little smaller than average.	Pelvis larger than average. Rib cage small in relation to pelvis.	Rib cage slightly large in relation to pelvis.	Rib cage large in relation to a small pelvis.
Which means . . .	you have a slightly "hippy" figure with a small, firm bustline.	you have a "hippy" figure with a bust that is proportionately small. You are probably tall.	your figure is fairly straight top to bottom with no accentuated curves.	your figure is "top-heavy" with slim hips and legs in relation to your full bust.
This means you tend to put on weight (in addition to your tummy . . .)	on your hips, thighs, and bottom.	on your hips, thighs, bottom. Watch your tummy—you could put on more than average here.	from the waist upwards—"spare tire", bust, underarms, shoulder blades. Watch your tummy, you may find this a problem spot.	from the waist upwards—on "spare tire", bust, underarms shoulder blades, tummy.
Your headaches are most likely to be . . .	your seat curve which could be aggravated by poor posture into an unattractive line.	heavy bottom, hips, thighs. Tendency to develop a tummy problem unless you keep those muscles trim. Heavy bones and flesh that make you weigh more than your figure seems to justify.	straight waist, a tendency to have a "spare tire", and a chance your bust might "drop".	tendency for your bust to "drop". "Spare-tire" and a fleshy back. You may also tend to be short-waisted.
You must watch out for these postural faults . . .	tendency to let your bottom stick out, giving an ugly buttock curve. Tuck it under and in.	you are probably inclined to be tall and may have the tall person's tendency to slump. Try always tucking your bottom in, as this will minimize your seat line.	no specific problem. Try always stretching up between bust and waist as this will help to make waist and diaphragm look slimmer.	none in particular, but always try to stand tall, elongating the body from the waist to the bust. This will improve the appearance of your figure tremendously.

It's the moment of truth. There is no fooling yourself, or your mirror image, when that zipper won't budge, or the buttons start popping. It is time for a sensible reducing diet. A moderate diet, preferably with medical guidance, will take those extra inches off gradually, and keep them off. You can watch the pounds slip away by checking your weight each week on the bathroom scales. Weigh yourself at the beginning of the day, when you are thinnest. If you have stuck to your diet, the noticeable weight loss will be an encouraging incentive to keep working at it.

body fat that is equivalent to another 1000 calories.

The average woman uses about 2000 calories going about her daily life—eight hours of work either in or outside the home, eight hours of recreation, and eight hours of sleep. The average man uses about 2700 calories if he is sedentary, and up to 3500 if he leads an active life. If you use up 2000 calories a day, and eat only 1000 calories in food, the remaining 1000 calories will come from your stored fat. Keeping to a 1000-calorie diet for one week can mean a weight loss of two pounds.

Here are some suggestions for turning your daily food allowances into appetizing meals. Remember that it's false economy to skip breakfast. Your body is at a low ebb first thing in the morning, and you need nourishment. Miss breakfast, and you're likely to be so ravenous by mid-morning that you can't resist the temptation to eat a candy bar or pastry as an energy boost.

Between meals you can have as many cups of coffee or tea as you like, provided you don't add sugar, and don't exceed your daily milk allowance. If you're still hungry and the next meal is some time away, try nibbling a raw carrot or celery. Hot drinks made of yeast or meat extract have virtually no calories at all, but are helpful in easing the pangs of hunger. You can substitute saccharin for sugar if you can't face coffee without sweetening. Liquid saccharin is handy to sprinkle on fresh fruit. Dilute it with a little fruit juice.

A 1000-calorie diet is a strict one, especially if you've been used to eating more than this, or if you have a sweet tooth. But you might have to eat still less—only 800 calories a day—if you are set on losing weight quickly. If you have this kind of will power, stay at 800 calories by keeping to the same menu given for the 1000-calorie diet, but substitute reconstituted low fat dried milk for fresh milk, and limit yourself to only one piece of fruit a day.

On 800 calories a day, you can expect a weight loss of $2\frac{1}{2}$ pounds a week. Don't try a

Dieting the 1,000 Calorie Way

Monday

Breakfast: 1 whole grapefruit, scrambled egg on toast, (1 oz. bread toasted with $\frac{1}{4}$ oz. butter)
Coffee

Lunch: Rollmop herring with salad bowl of lettuce, cucumber, chicory, and celery. Garnish with orange slices
Baked apple, coffee.

Dinner: Fruit juice cocktail, 3 oz. spareribs with applesauce (unsweetened)
French beans, beets.
Cheese with celery and carrot sticks.
Tea with lemon.

Tuesday

Breakfast: Wedge of melon, 2 oz. lean bacon broiled with tomatoes and mushrooms.
Coffee or tea.

Lunch: Spanish omelet (2 eggs with 1 cup of mixed vegetables, excluding potato).
Citrus fruit salad, coffee.

Dinner: Grilled grapefruit. 2 oz. diced cheese with a mixed salad or cucumber, radishes, sweet peppers, celery and watercress, 1 oz. French bread with $\frac{1}{4}$ oz. butter.
Coffee

Wednesday

Breakfast: Plain yogurt with sliced banana, boiled egg with 1 slice of wholewheat bread, and $\frac{1}{4}$ oz. butter.
Tea with lemon.

Lunch: 4 oz. broiled liver and tomatoes, broccoli spears.
Fresh apple, coffee.

Dinner: Small fillet of whitefish topped with 1 oz. of melted cheese. Baked zucchini, peas.
4 oz. bunch of black grapes, coffee.

Thursday

Breakfast: Cranberry juice, bacon omelet (1 egg with 1 oz. bacon), 1 small muffin with $\frac{1}{4}$ oz. butter.
Coffee.

Lunch: Mixed vegetable soup (not thickened) topped with 1 oz. finely grated cheese. Shrimps on a bed of lettuce with crispbread.
Small glass milk.

Dinner: Broiled chicken with banana, salad bowl of lettuce, endive, and chopped chives with lemon juice dressing. Pears baked in orange juice and nutmeg.
Coffee.

Friday

Breakfast: Tomato juice cocktail, slice wholewheat bread with thin slice cold ham and thin slice of cheese.
Coffee.

Lunch: 1 lean 3 oz. hamburger with spinach and tomatoes.
Apple, small glass milk.

Dinner: 2 curried eggs, side salads of tomato and onion, sliced green peppers, celery, and banana slices sprinkled with lemon juice.
Chilled orange segments.
Tea.

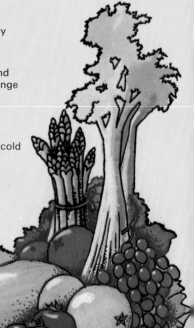

Left: a 1000-calorie diet isn't as close to a mild starvation course as you might think it is. These suggested menus for five days include plenty of different and tasty foods to satisfy your normal appetite.

Right: breakfast is the dieter's most important meal. Start the day well with a delicious, slimming breakfast of soft-boiled egg, lightly buttered rye or wheat crisp crackers, an apple, and coffee with some milk.

more drastic scale of dieting. Even on 800 calories, you will be paring down your nutrient intake to the lowest limit. You may be one of those people who need more protein, or more of some vitamins and minerals. To cut down your calories too far can mean that you are damaging your body tissues. You will get that irritable, worn-out feeling many people associate with dieting. Your looks are likely to suffer, too.

There are many crash diets that promise you a remarkable weight loss in only a few days. These diets are often based on only two or three different foods, such as milk and bananas, yogurt and celery, or cottage cheese and fruit. The idea is that you eat nothing but these foods for every meal. You will probably find that you can lose weight on a diet like this.

However, if you can stick to such a limited menu at all, your weight loss during the first few days will likely be due entirely to change in the body's water balance. But it's loss of fat that proper dieting is all about. Remember that any diet which restricts food variety and total food severely cannot

be a well-balanced diet. Your body's need for proteins, minerals, and vitamins will not be supplied, and if you keep to a crash diet for any length of time, your health is bound to suffer.

There is a more relaxed way to diet. Many people find it is a much better policy to stick to a diet that is not too rigid, even if it means staying on the diet longer to lose the desired amount of weight. A 1200- or 1500-calorie diet is much easier to adhere to, because you can allow yourself a few small helpings of carbohydrate foods. You should still concentrate on eating enough of the right foods for good health, but you are allowed greater variety through the addition of some starches, fruits, and desserts. As long as the extra 100 calories are in the foods that do not increase the energy value of the diet, you will probably not feel the least bit cheated. That is, unless you have an uncontrollable sweet tooth.

Giving up sugar is a challenge. You feel just as deprived as a smoker trying to give up cigarettes. But self-control will pay off, and you'll find that you'll lose the taste for sweet things after a time.

All dieters are advised to give up sugar. But if you have decided on a 1200- or 1500-calorie diet, you can allow yourself some carbohydrates in the form of starchy foods, such as bread, crackers, rice, spaghetti, or potatoes. On a 1200-calorie diet you can allow yourself two 100-calorie portions of starchy foods.

For the 200 calories added to the basic 1000-calorie diet you could have: two slices of bread thinly spread with butter; or four starch reduced crackers with a bit of butter; or a bowl of cereal and one thin slice of unbuttered bread; or a medium-sized baked potato; or five ounces of boiled new potatoes with one thin slice of unbuttered bread. Keeping to 1200 calories a day, you can expect a weight loss of about 1½ pounds each week.

A 1500-calorie diet should be easy to keep to. Most people find it is what they are eating presently, minus all the sweet foods in their diet. In addition to your daily allowance of protein foods, fruit, and vegetables, you can choose five 100-calorie portions of starchy foods. You may prefer to increase your protein foods instead of allowing yourself more starchy foods. While there is a lower limit to the amount of meat, milk, fish, and eggs you need to eat, you can eat as much of them as you like, provided you do not exceed your daily 1500 calories in your total food intake.

If you have more than 15 pounds to lose, you're best advised to keep to the 1500-calorie diet. Although you may lose only one pound a week on the average, you do not have to restrict your food intake severely. If you have a lot of weight to lose, it means that you have been eating too much for a long time. It is too much of a shock to have to cut back drastically to only 1000 calories a day. Many people start off on a strict diet,

Left: quite a change from your former chubbier self! After a long-term effort to slim down your figure, you won't mind investing in some new clothes that will show off your new figure to best advantage. Crash diets might achieve the same results in less time, but the sudden weight loss is unhealthy, and the pounds come right back.

Above: if you are following a 1200- to 1500-calorie diet, you can afford to include some starches in your daily count. Each of these portions of starchy foods equals 100 calories: five ounces boiled potatoes; four crisp rye or wheat crackers; three ounces pasta; four ounces butter beans; one medium-size roll; eight ounces peas; 1½ ounces wholemeal bread; one ounce breakfast cereal.
Left: artificial sweeteners have no calories at all.

but give it up quickly, feeling rotten after their short trial period. It is much better to diet slowly but surely, so that your appetite can readjust to the smaller amount of food. Your skin and flesh find it easier to shrink back over a smaller body frame. Muscles that have been stretched over pounds of fat need time to recover their elasticity and muscle tone.

If you have a daily calorie budget of 1500 calories, you can allow yourself a small lapse now and again, without feeling your diet has been ruined. An important note—the weeks spent in losing weight slowly but surely re-educate your palate. So think of the whole dieting period as a long-term investment.

For many people, weight control must be

a lifelong job. When you have lost weight, it is just as important to keep your reduced weight. Usually if you have slimmed successfully on a 1500-calorie diet, you will find you can eat a few hundred calories more and still keep to your new weight. If the weight starts to build up again, it is back to the 1500 calories a day for a week or two.

Isn't there an easier way to diet? Many people rely, perhaps psychologically, on reducing garments, exercise machines, and sauna baths. But we can say unequivocally that there is only one way to lose weight, and that is by cutting down on the food you eat. Scientists are trying to develop a pill that burns off all your excess fat, but it has not yet been perfected. Some of the other reducing devices may help, but some of them do no good at all. The reducing garments that make you sweat, the sauna, or the Turkish bath may bring a small weight loss. But it is only short-lived, because it is due to loss of water from the body. Have a drink of water, and you've regained those ounces you lost.

Exercise, on the other hand, helps in weight reduction, because it increases the rate at which you burn off your body fat. But it is almost impossible to lose weight by exercise alone. You wouldn't have enough time in the day to do the exercise necessary to make an appreciable difference in your weight. But taking a regular amount of exercise every day is one of the basic rules for health and vitality. Exercise also maintains muscle tone, and helps the body to regulate food intake by means of the appetite. The appetite breaks down as a controlling mechanism when you have too little exercise.

What about cutting down on carbohydrates to lose weight? If you take the basic daily allowances of the foods described for the 1000-calorie diet, you will find they are also low in carbohydrate. In the 1000-calorie diet, you would be getting sugar in your fruit and in the daily allowance of milk. Depending on the type of fruit you choose— bananas and grapes are high in carbohydrate, apples are medium, and peaches and pineapple are low—you would have roughly

Left: dieting will take off the pounds, but what do you do about the excess flabbiness left? An exercise program will tone your muscles, and also give you an overall feeling of good health. If you are really enthusiastic about getting in shape, you may want to join an exercise class.

Below: many people practice yoga for fitness and muscle tone.

Right: sauna baths are a relaxing means of sweating away excess body fluid, but any loss of weight is temporary.

30 grams of fruit sugar. In the half pint daily allowance of milk, you would take another 16 grams of carbohydrate. Together this amounts to 46 grams of carbohydrate. On most low carbohydrate diets, the daily allowance is between 50 and 60 grams, so you see how the calorie controlled 1000-calorie diet is also a low carbohydrate diet, and vice versa.

In theory, the low carbohydrate diet allows you to eat as much protein and fat as you like, clamping down only on carbohydrates. According to this diet, there is no restriction on meat, fish, or poultry, provided it is not cooked in carbohydrate-rich pastry, batters, or sauces. You can eat as much cheese, butter, margarine, and eggs as you wish, provided they are not in any dish in which flour, potato, or other carbohydrate-rich ingredients are used. That means that foods such as meat loaf, sausage, and breaded chops, which are made with flour or another cereal product, are forbidden.

How can you eat all you want of protein and fat, and still hope to lose weight? In practice, there is a limit to the amount of these foods you can eat, especially when the quantity of carbohydrate foods is cut down to a bare minimum. You will find it is uninteresting to eat more than one boiled egg without toast, or a steak without potatoes. When it comes down to it, the low carbohydrate diet is also a calorie controlled diet. You just can't lose weight without cutting down on your total energy intake from foods, whichever way you choose to do it.

Generally speaking, the low carbohydrate diet is an easy one to stick to. Provided you keep an account of how many carbohydrate grams you're eating daily, and you know which of our normal range of foods are richest in carbohydrates, you don't have to bother with counting the calories in everything you eat. The chart on page 93 will help you.

When the low carbohydrate diet was introduced years ago, many people were surprised that there was no restriction on the amount of fat they could eat while dieting. A journalist coined the phrase "eat fat and grow slim". At face value this could be taken to mean that the more fat you eat, the slimmer you become. Of course, this is not true. Fat is high in calories. One ounce of butter contains 226 calories. Luckily, fatty foods are filling, so you cannot eat too much of them. Even so, to lose weight at a reasonable rate, it is wise to cut down on high-calorie, rich foods. Even if you cut out pastries, cakes, mayonnaise, and similar fatty foods, and trim most of the fat off your meat, you will still be eating a fair amount of fat in its invisible form.

Invisible fat is the fat in cheese, milk, and eggs, and the fat that is found even in seemingly lean meat. A low fat diet can leave you hungry, because fats make a meal more satisfying. More important, certain vitamins are found only in the fat of some foods. So a low fat diet may be short of vitamins A, D, or E. A low carbohydrate diet allows you to have more fat than a low calorie diet, and therefore may be more enjoyable, as well as easier, for some people.

Although we hear such a lot these days about overweight and dieting, very few people bother themselves with the problems of the "skinnies". People who are excessively underweight, especially teenagers and young adults, are often acutely aware of their thinness. Despite the fact that fashion was never kinder to the very thin than it is today, the over-thin may still feel that their thinness is unattractive. They feel angular and gawky. It is no use telling a thin person that he or she is much healthier than someone who is overweight, that millions of people spend weeks deprived of delicious food just to get thin, and that millions of dollars are spent each year on diet aids. They are as sensitive about their weight as a fat person. Have you ever noticed that, while few people would remark on a person's fatness, most people think nothing of saying, "My! Aren't you thin!", or "However do you stay as thin as that?"

Although almost any person who is fat can lose weight by the right type of reducing diet, some thin people are almost impossible to fatten up. It just seems that the thin can't overcome their high metabolism. If they eat more food than they need for their day's energy, they burn up the excess with not an ounce left over to pad out their bones. Experiments with overfeeding young active adults have proven this. Even though the subjects ate over 500 calories a day more than they needed for their individual energy requirements, the excess was not converted into stored body fat as it would be by a person who was prone to overweight. A natural fatty would quickly convert this daily 500 calories surplus into one full pound of body fat in a week.

Some thin people eat enormous amounts, and never get any fatter. There is very little they can do to put on weight except to try to take life more slowly. The message to them must be "Walk, don't run". If they could slow down, they might have some surplus calories that could be changed into body fat. A relaxing, sedentary hobby for one or two evenings a week can help, although a thin person who is active often finds it nearly impossible to sit still for any length of time. If you eat plenty, if you have a consistent good appetite and eat well-balanced meals, and if you still cannot put on an ounce of

Watch those Carbohydrates

On a low carbohydrate diet, you are allowed a maximum of 60 carbohydrate grams daily. A gram-counter could eat a dinner of: honeydew melon wedge—13 grams, with prosciutto ham—0; 3 spears broccoli—4, with hollandaise sauce—0; lobster tail with butter sauce—0; romaine lettuce with Roquefort dressing—0; glass white wine—1; vanilla ice cream with chocolate sauce—15; coffee with cream—1. This totals 37 grams. With a substantial breakfast, and a light protein lunch, no active person could complain about such a generous diet.

Here are just a few of the foods to stay away from on a low-carbohydrate diet. Remember that most high protein foods—meat, fish, eggs, butter, oils, and alcoholic beverages—have hardly any carbohydrate count.

Fruit	grams
apple, 1 raw	18
apricots, 2 dried	13
banana, 1	35
cherries, 1 cup canned	59
cranberries, 1 cup	11
grapefruit, ½ fresh	22
pear, 1 fresh	24
1 cup canned	50
plums, 1 cup canned	50

Vegetables	
beans, 1 cup cooked lima	29
1 cup cooked kidney	42
1 cup baked	48
beets, 1 cup	16
carrots, 1 cup	10
corn, 1 ear	24
peas, ½ cup frozen	11
1 lb. fresh	36
potatoes, 1 baked	22
½ cup fried	31

Alcoholic Beverages	
beer, 8 oz.	11
port, 3½ oz.	14
rum and cola, average	20
vermouth, 3½ oz.	12

Cereal Products	grams
shredded wheat biscuit, 1	18
bran flakes, 1 cup	28
corn flakes, 1 cup	21
raisin bran, 1 cup	33
rolled cooked oats, 1 cup	40
white bread, 1 slice	12
wheat bread, 1 slice	11
cornbread, 1 slice	21
macaroni, 1 cup cooked	32
egg noodles, 1 cup	37
white rice, 1 cup cooked	44
soda cracker, 1	4
rye crispbread, 1	10
barley, 1 cup dry	120
wheat germ, 1 cup	34
cashews, ½ cup	20
almonds, ½ cup	13

Desserts	
chocolate pudding, ½ cup	31
rice pudding, ½ cup	17
apple pie, 1 slice	47
berry pie, 1 slice	43
lemon meringue pie, 1 slice	39
two-layer cake, 1 slice	54
Danish pastry, 1	41
chocolate ice cream, ¼ pt.	17

weight, you must accept that you are one of the world's thin ones.

Take comfort from the fact that you can eat practically anything you like. Just think now and then about all the fatties who are doomed to a life of self-denial of the foods they love that you can eat and enjoy. If you are still under 25, you can also hope that after that age, your metabolism will slow down, and you may find that you have a few more feminine curves. Many underweight under 25's find that they reach average weight in their 30's or 40's.

If you are thin largely because you have a poor appetite, there is much more that you can do to put on weight. First of all, have a talk with your doctor. There may be some vitamin or mineral pills that can correct a minor deficiency. If you are one of the worrying kind, your doctor may suggest sedatives or pills that will help you relax to get more sleep, and more refreshing sleep.

Have you ever sat down to a meal feeling hungry, but found that your appetite disappeared as you took the first bite? If this happens to you, change from the usual three meals a day, and go for five or six smaller meals instead. You must make sure that each snack is well-balanced, containing some protein and some fresh fruit, salad, or vegetables. You should never have only high carbohydrate snacks, and always have small portions of everything. It is no good trying to make yourself eat by piling food on your plate. Large helpings in themselves often scare away a small appetite still further.

Next, try to avoid very rich and fatty foods. It sounds like a contradiction in terms to cut out fattening foods if you want to put on

weight. But what actually happens is that very rich foods also reduce a small appetite. You get full too quickly if you have a fried chop, a portion of fried fish in batter, or broiled meat covered with a thick creamy sauce. Go for the more refreshing, lighter dishes instead. Have a salad with your meal, but don't choose a mayonnaise or other creamy dressing. A piquant French or lemon dressing complements most foods.

A small appetizer of salad, hors d'oeuvre, tomato juice, consomme, or grapefruit or melon also stimulates the appetite. Always avoid heavy appetizers, such as thick soups or pâtés. You will be full long before you reach the main course. Bitter foods, such as olives, or nonsweet aperitifs also help to stimulate the appetite.

You can have drink with the meal, but in moderation. Many thin people are advised not to drink with a meal because it "fills them up," but some find it hard to swallow food, or at least to enjoy food, when thirsty. Choose milk to drink if you like it because it can help to put on weight. If you prefer, have a glass of beer, or a glass of wine. Choose dry wines rather than sweet ones. Dryness of wine stimulates the flow of digestive juices, while sweetness makes you feel full halfway through the meal by signaling the end of the meal.

Always try to eat in relaxed, pleasant surroundings, and don't rush through a meal. Try to allow a full hour so that you can have a quarter of an hour or so of relaxation over a cup of coffee after the meal. If you eat in a hurry, and jump up as soon as you have finished the last bite, is it any wonder that you will be burning up your food almost

94

before you have gotten any good out of it?

Eating breakfast while working, which has become a habit with executives over the last decade, is one of the worst ideas going for the underweight—and, incidentally, for the high powered executives who suffer from ulcers. Having a business lunch also means that you are working while eating, and this unrelaxed atmosphere is not advisable if you want to gain weight. However, if you must have a working meal, choose dishes that are easily digested. Skip exotic foods swimming in butter or rich sauces for a simple broiled or roast meat, with a little mashed or creamed potatoes, vegetables, or salad. Have just one glass of wine.

Whether it is yourself or your husband that you are trying to fatten, remember that a long-term effort to change eating habits may reward you with a few extra pounds.

95

Dieting Because You Must

6

Food, glorious food! Most of us love it. Many people would go so far as to consider food as one of the greatest pleasures of life. Rare, juicy steaks, pork chops, roast duckling, and fried chicken; oysters and other shellfish, such as lobster and crab; sauces rich with cream and eggs; salads with various dressings; rich pastries and chocolates—these are the kinds of food most people would rank as their favorites. It is a well-established fact that as our standing of living goes up, we shun plain starches such as bread and potatoes, and we choose instead high protein foods, and foods that contain a high proportion of animal fats.

In the past, doctors have claimed that a diet high in protein and fat, and low in carbohydrates, was the best one. More recently, this blanket kind of approval, which recommends the same type of diet to everyone, is falling into disrepute. There are still some influential and vocal advocates of the high fat diet, but most medical opinion seems to oppose this. For their health's sake, there are many people who should not increase their fat consumption; in fact, they would be healthier, and less prone to crippling heart diseases, if they were to reduce the fat they eat.

To certain people, the type of food they eat is really a matter of life and death. When we speak of a diet to prevent disease, we usually mean heart disease. But there are thousands of people who must watch their intake of salt and sugar as carefully as a person with a history of heart disease. A diabetic may have to limit his carbohydrates to actual gram measurement, and avoid all sugar consumption. Patients on low sodium

Celebrating your fiftieth birthday in excellent health depends much on a lifetime of good eating habits and adequate exercise. Grim medical statistics show that overweight tends not only to shorten your life span, but also to make you a target for related heart diseases and diabetes.

The Early Warning Signs of Heart Attack

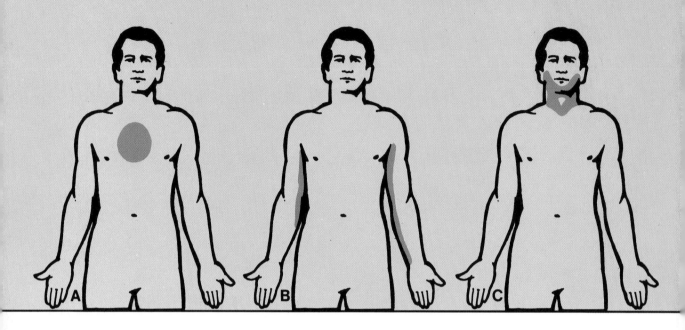

A. The most usual pain caused by a heart attack is not a sharp, jabbing pain, but a feeling of pressure, aching, or fullness in the center of the chest. This is actually the location of the heart, and not the left side as most people believe. The sensation is caused by a lack of oxygen in the heart muscle. The pain may be mild to severe; it can be centered, or it can radiate throughout the chest; it may last a few minutes, or a few hours, and it may recur days or weeks later. B. Discomfort may extend from the chest into one or both arms, or may be only in the arms. It is often mistaken for arthritis, bursitis, or simply muscle strain. To help determine the cause, raise your arms above the head. Arthritic or bursitic pain can be aggravated by this movement, but heart pain will not. C. Distress may radiate into any part of the neck and jaws. To check

or low cholesterol diets may, like the diabetic, be on medication to help them lead a normal life. But it is their carefully planned diet more than medication that keeps them out of danger.

In the past, doctors and nutritionists have considered the food we eat in terms of carbohydrates, fats, protein, minerals, and vitamins. Now we know that the *kind* of carbohydrate you eat is important. We also know that the *constituents* of the many different types of fat in your diet, and the actual proportions of them normally supplied in your food, are other vitally important nutritional factors. The reason they are so important is that several dietary factors appear to be closely related to heart diseases, and other diseases of the circulatory system.

Every year, about one million people in the United States die from *cardiovascular diseases*. More than half of these deaths are caused by *arteriosclerotic heart disease*. Cardiovascular disease claims more victims than any other single cause of death. Not everyone dies as the result of an attack, but every year 600,000 people become seriously ill as a result of heart disease. The incidence of these killing or crippling diseases is not exceeded anywhere else in the world, although similar figures can be found in all affluent countries of the western world. The victims are most frequently men over 40 years of age. Unless they suffer from high blood pressure or diabetes, women do not appear to be as susceptible to heart diseases until they have passed menopause. It may be that the female sex hormones protect women in some way.

Understandably, a great deal of time and

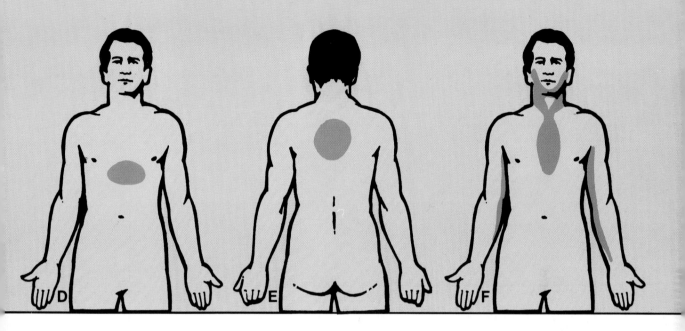

if the pain could be due to arthritis, toothache, or just a stiff neck, turn your head or bend your neck. The heart pain will not be aggravated by the movement, but pain originating in the neck will be. D. Another sign can be aching or squeezing pain in the upper abdomen overlapping the lower chest at the fork of the ribs. It can be mistaken for indigestion, especially because nausea or vomiting may also occur. E. Back pain between the shoulder blades may be the only sign of a heart attack; it is often confused with muscular strain. F. Distress can be in a combination of areas, such as chest and arms, or chest, neck, and jaws. It may be accompanied by nausea, vomiting, shortness of breath, and particularly heavy cold sweating. Unexplained sweating, if associated with pain in these areas, is usually considered to be a sign of a heart attack.

Don't be misled by these chest pains that are usually harmless. G., H. A pain in the left chest wall, centering on the left nipple, is almost never a sign of heart attack. The pain may be sharp, jabbing, and last for only a few seconds, or it may be a dull soreness lasting minutes or hours, or a combination of both. Many persons who are normally tense experience this type of pain frequently, mistaking it for a heart attack. If the discomfort continues, you should always see your doctor.

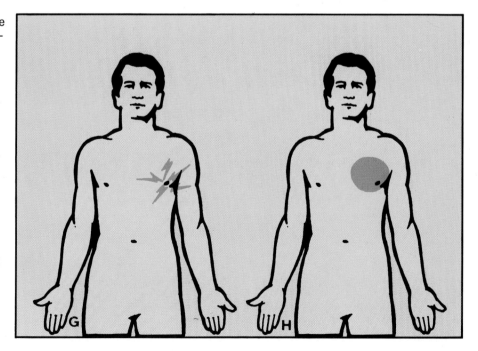

Heart Disease -
Some Medical Terms Explained

Atheroma—porridge-like deposits made up of cholesterol, other fatty materials, complex carbohydrates, blood, and blood products. The deposits stick to the inside of the artery walls. Eventually, the deposits may cause atherosclerosis.

Atherosclerosis—develops as the atheroma collect on the inside of the arteries, congesting the arteries, and restricting the flow of blood. In severe cases, the lumen of the artery is almost closed. When this happens, the blood supply slows down. Blood cells get stuck in the arteries, and often form themselves into a clot or thrombus. Atherosclerosis is often known as "hardening of the arteries".

Cholesterol—a fatty substance found in all animal tissues. Its job in the blood is to carry fats through the body.

Blood cholesterol level—the actual amount of cholesterol found in the blood. This varies in different people, but the higher the level, the more susceptible the individual to a heart attack, or coronary thrombosis. Men with a cholesterol level higher than 230* suffer three times the number of attacks as men with cholesterol levels below 210. In any one person, the blood cholesterol level tends to increase with age.
*230 mg Cholesterol in 100 ml of blood.

Coronary arteries—the blood vessels that carry blood to the heart muscle itself.

Coronary thrombosis—a heart attack caused by a clot of blood blocking off one of the coronary arteries. When blood flow is restricted in this way, part of the heart muscle may cease to function entirely. The severity of the heart attack depends on the area of the heart muscle that was cut off from its life-giving blood supply.

Fatty acids—one of the constituents of the fats we eat in food. Each molecule of the fatty acid is like a chain, or a ring, of carbon atoms to which hydrogen and oxygen atoms are attached. Some fatty acids have less than their full quota of hydrogen atoms. These fatty acids are described as being *unsaturated fatty acids.* Vegetable oils contain more unsaturated fatty acids than animal fats.

Monounsaturated fatty acids—fatty acids in which two adjacent carbon atoms are short of hydrogen.

Polyunsaturated fatty acids—sometimes known as "polyunsaturates" or PUFA; fatty acids in which two or more pairs of carbon atoms have less than their full quota of hydrogen.

Essential fatty acids—two or three (nutritionists are uncertain on this point) unsaturated fatty acids that are vital for good health, but cannot be made in the body. They must come ready-made in our daily food.

Lipid—the medical term used to describe all fats and fat-like substances in the body. Blood lipids, then, are fats carried in the blood.

Thrombus—a blood clot formed within the blood vessels.

Thrombosis—the restriction of blood supply to certain tissues of the body caused by the blood vessels being blocked by a thrombus or clot.

Triglycerides—three fatty acid molecules combined with one molecule of glycerol make triglycerides. The triglycerides are then linked together to make the complex molecules of fat. During digestion of fats, the long complex molecules are broken down to their constituents. As free fatty acids and monoglycerides, the fats pass into the blood system. There they are joined together to make triglycerides. Normally blood proteins link with the triglycerides so they will dissolve in the blood for transport round the body. If the fat intake is abnormally high, or if the blood proteins are unable to make the usual linkage with the triglycerides, free triglycerides will float in the blood.

Left: with so much written and said about heart disease, you may find it helpful to know some common medical terms used in relation to it.

Right: eating his way to a possible heart attack, or other serious illnesses, this obese man is one of a growing number in the United States. Gross overweight leads to high risk of coronary thrombosis, high blood pressure, diabetes, impotence, and infertility.

money is devoted to research to find the cause of cardiovascular diseases. The results so far show that there is not one single cause, but many factors that appear to be closely linked. Most research shows that the major risk factors are: high blood pressure level; high blood *cholesterol*; high *triglyceride* (fat) levels in the blood; lack of exercise and obesity; mental stress; cigarette smoking; diabetes; and family history of heart disease.

Some of these are obviously related. For example, many people become severely overweight when they eat too much rich food. The same rich foods, especially sugar and fats, appear to affect the blood cholesterol level. Problems of overweight may be accentuated by inactivity, while physical exercise itself seems to have some protective effect against a heart complaint. People under considerable mental stress often have high blood pressure, smoke heavily, and allow themselves little time for physical exercise.

Heredity increasingly plays a major part in the development of heart disease. How fat is carried in your blood, and what its cholesterol level is, often follow a family pattern. Scientists and nutritionists call fats *lipids*. The blood carries these lipids to the body tissues to provide us with a quick source of energy. Lipids are not soluble in blood, so normally they are linked together with blood proteins—like harnessing a horse to a carriage. When they are linked together they form *lipoproteins*, which are carried around the body dissolved in the blood. A small proportion of people are born with defective mechanisms for carrying blood. In their blood, lipids float free. This condition can be just as influential in causing heart disease as a high cholesterol level.

The most common fats are the true, or neutral, fats that make up 90 per cent of all food and body fats. True fats are made up of many smaller units known as *triglycerides*. Triglycerides are simply glycerol attached to three fatty acids—like our lipoproteins carriage, but this time with three horses. The fatty acids may be all the same, or they may be different ones. There are three types of fatty acids: saturated, monounsaturated, and polyunsaturated. You can eat some form of these fatty acids every day in butter, margarine, cooking oil, cheese, some vegetables, cereals, and meat. It is the amount you consume that makes the difference.

The National Heart and Lung Institute at the National Institutes of Health in Bethesda, Md., strongly recommends that patients be screened not only for blood cholesterol levels, but for triglyceride levels as well. If either of these are above normal, there is a danger that a person may one day suffer from a coronary thrombosis. Also, if your parents or grandparents died early of a heart attack, there is a strong chance that you will have inherited their susceptibility to cardiovascular diseases. If you are diabetic, you are even more prone to cardiovascular diseases, especially heart attacks.

Those who die from a coronary thrombosis are always found to have been suffering from severe *atherosclerosis*, which involves the accumulation of *atheroma*, or fatty deposits. Because they don't have enough conclusive scientific proof, doctors cannot lay the blame for developing atheroma unreservedly on the high level of cholesterol and free lipids in the blood. But there is strong circumstantial evidence that cholesterol and free lipids do contribute to the dangerous fatty deposits. It is obviously a safeguard to keep the blood cholesterol and triglyceride levels as low as possible. This is essential for anyone who has already suffered a mild heart attack, or has been warned by his doctor that he is a likely coronary candidate unless special precautions are taken.

You can make substantial changes in the blood cholesterol levels by altering your sugar and fat intake, substituting vegetable oils for some of the animals fats, and drinking skim milk instead of whole milk. The more total fat you eat, the higher the level of triglycerides your blood will carry, if you are one of the unfortunate minority who

When your doctor advises you to go on a low fat or low cholesterol diet, you should concentrate on eating foods that have a high percentage of unsaturated fatty acids. This chart gives you some common foods, and their breakdown into saturated and unsaturated fats. You will see that the all-American food favorite, steak, is a meat to be avoided—it is only 51 per cent unsaturated fat. Of the meats, poultry is the best bet on helping you keep down your saturated fat intake; it is 75 per cent unsaturated fat. You will also see that margarine is better on low fat diets than butter, and safflower or corn oil better than olive oil. A switch to skimmed milk is called for if you must watch your fat intake.

Finding the Fats

	Total fat content by Grams	Saturated fat by Grams	% of total fat that is unsaturated fatty acids
bacon – 2 slices or 2 oz.	8	3	62
sirloin steak, fat and lean – 3 oz.	27	13	51
roast leg lamb – 3 oz.	16	9	43
pork chop, fat and lean – 3½ oz. (weighed with bone)	21	8	62
chicken drumstick – 2 oz.	4	1	75
1 cup whole milk	9	5	33
1 oz. hard cheese	9	5	33
4 oz. cottage cheese	4.7	2.7	43
1 egg	6	2	66
1 tablespoon peanut butter	8	2	75
,, ,, butter	12	6	50
,, ,, lard	13	5	62
,, ,, vegetable shortening	13	3	77
,, ,, regular margarine	12	2	83
,, ,, soft margarine	11	2	82
,, ,, corn oil	14	1	93
,, ,, cotton seed oil	14	4	71
,, ,, olive oil	14	2	86
,, ,, peanut oil	14	3	79
,, ,, safflower oil	14	1	93
,, ,, soya bean oil	14	2	86

suffer from an impaired fat-carrying mechanism.

Remember that atherosclerosis does not build up overnight. Deposits develop slowly over the years. But don't wait until they build up to dangerous levels before you take action. It is never too early to start taking precautions against atherosclerosis, because food habits develop early. We get set into eating and liking certain foods. If we have to make drastic changes later in life, it can seem like a real hardship.

You can start in a simple way by making sure that your husband and children are not carrying excess weight. Overweight people are much more susceptible to heart attacks than people who are of average weight. Encourage your family to take plenty of exercise. If your husband has an exacting job that keeps him working under constant mental stress, get him to relax in the evenings—not slumped in an armchair, but on a pleasant walk, or a gentle round of golf. Set them all a good example by not smoking,

Sporadic bursts of strenuous activity wear you out, and may have an adverse effect on your health. Regular, moderate exercise will help you to prevent a heart attack, or to keep you more physically fit if you have a history of heart disease. Pick a relaxing and steady form of activity that gets you into the fresh air. An easy nine holes of golf, some hours at the fishing spot, or fifteen minutes of jogging eases everyday tensions, and keeps your muscles toned and active.

and do your best to steer them away from cigarettes.

In some diseases, particularly heart complaints and toxemia, water seems to be retained in the body. If this is allowed to continue unchecked, the blood pressure may rise alarmingly, causing serious complications. If someone is recovering from a heart attack, a rise in blood pressure can bring on another attack.

In a pregnant woman, increased blood pressure can cause damage to the unborn baby, because the supply of blood to the baby is partially closed off. Fortunately, water retention is usually spotted long before these troubles occur. Then a low sodium, or a low salt, diet is recommended to cure the problem of carrying excess water.

Various degrees of sodium restriction may be prescribed. These depend on the severity of the condition. Very often, a person is just forbidden to eat any food cooked with extra salt. He mustn't add salt at the table, and must keep away from any food with a high

105

sodium content. A more severe condition may mean that a person can eat only those foods with a naturally low sodium content, and, of course, food cooked and eaten without added salt. A low sodium diet is not very often recommended to someone at home, because he will need constant supervision. He is, therefore, usually kept under a doctor's or dietician's eyes in the hospital. Occasionally, a heavily restricted diet is prescribed for only a few days for a person at home. Because it is for a short time, it is often simpler to rely on foods that are manufactured especially for this type of diet instead of cooking every meal yourself.

To safeguard the dieter if you do the cooking, you can either cook all the food unsalted, remove the dieter's portion, and salt the rest for other members of the family; or you can serve it all unsalted, and let each person salt his portion at the table to suit his own taste. Check with your doctor to determine whether the ill person is allowed to use a salt substitute in place of normal table salt. If it is allowed, the substitute will make meals much more palatable. It is surprising how insipid most foods taste without salt to enhance the other flavoring ingredients.

Food for Your Heart's Sake

HIGH CHOLESTEROL FOODS

▶ There are some foods that are high in cholesterol and should be avoided, or at least severely restricted, by heart patients. Cholesterol is found only in certain animal foods, and is highly concentrated in organ meats. Therefore, it is better to limit your intake of liver, kidney, brains, and sweetbreads. Avoid certain shellfish, including lobster, and also fish roe. Follow the American Medical Association's recommendation, and serve no more than three eggs per week to anyone with a heart condition. Don't allow more than one egg daily for the rest of the family.

ANIMAL FATS

▶ Animal fats tend to raise the blood cholesterol level. Most common sources of saturated fats are butter, cream, fat meats, such as pork and ham, and the outside fat of otherwise lean meats, such as beef and lamb. Hard cheese, cream cheese, and whole milk are also high in saturated fats. Try substituting vegetable margarine for butter in cooking and table use. Choose lean meats, and switch to skim milk in place of whole milk. Use non-dairy cream, in moderation, for coffee.

If a salt substitute is not permitted, make full use of herbs and spices to add flavor to the diet dishes. Be careful, of course, about using prepared flavoring ingredients. Some of them are laden with monosodium glutamate (MSG), a flavor enhancer, which is just as harmful as salt. Always check the list of ingredients on the label before serving any kind of convenience food to see if salt or MSG is included.

Remember that most commonly used leavening or raising agents are sodium salts. Self-rising flour, then, is definitely out when you're preparing a low sodium diet. You must not use cake mixes, or any mixes that incorporate a leavening agent. A pharmacist should be able to sell you a sodium-free baking powder to use in place of the ones normally available. Use this special powder with plain flour to substitute for self-rising flour, or in other recipes calling for baking powder.

Diabetes is a disease that makes the body unable to select carbohydrates from food and convert them into energy. The body produces the hormone insulin for proper utilization of carbohydrates, but in diabetes, there is a breakdown of the mechanism that

VEGETABLE OILS AND FATS

▶ Some vegetable oils contain more polyunsaturates than others. Polyunsaturated vegetable oils help to lower blood cholesterol levels. Choose sunflower, cottonseed, corn, or peanut oils. Most soft margarines are high in polyunsaturated fats; check this on the label. Use oil or margarine for cooking in place of butter. You can fry in the oils listed above, but cut out fried foods as far as possible. Beware of coconut oil and products made with it, including some non-dairy products. The fats in coconut oil are saturated, and not good for the heart patient.

SUGAR

▶ Sugar also seems to have a bad effect in raising blood cholesterol levels. Cut out sugar as far as possible. Substitute saccharin for use in coffee and tea. You can also use liquid saccharin in cooked foods, but add it after the food has been fully cooked to avoid a bitter taste. Cut down on all desserts, cakes, cookies, bought bakery goods, and other foods with a high sugar content. Be especially careful of the sugar hidden in packaged foods of many kinds.

produces insulin. After carbohydrates are digested in the normal way, they pass from the intestine into the blood stream in the form of glucose. Normally, each part of the body requiring oxygen makes use of insulin to help burn this important fuel or source of energy. With a shortage, or a complete lack of insulin, the glucose builds up in the blood. It is finally disposed of by the kidney, and passes unused out of the body in the urine. That is why the test for glucose in the urine is one of the routine checks for diabetes.

Diabetes is often caused by eating a high carbohydrate diet for a long period. This is one reason why diabetes is found more commonly among overweight people than in people of average weight. When the body is called on to deal with an overload of food, year in and year out, the cells that produce the insulin simply become worn-out by overwork. They may cut down on their output of insulin, or stop functioning completely. Many women also find they suffer a mild form of diabetes when they become pregnant.

Nowadays, most diabetics can lead perfectly normal lives provided they stick to the treatment prescribed by their doctors. This generally involves taking regular doses of insulin or other like medication, and restricting the carbohydrate intake severely. It means a strict control on the diet at all times. Even so, a person can keep the fact that he's diabetic from his best friend, if he wants to, because he can live so normally.

In mild cases of diabetes, a controlled carbohydrate intake alone is sufficient treatment. In more severe cases, insulin—either as tablets or daily injections—is required. When insulin is taken, it is just as important that the carbohydrate intake be carefully balanced so that there is enough glucose in the blood to make use of the insulin. Too much carbohydrate will make some of the glucose pass over into the urine, and too little carbohydrate will make the glucose level fall drastically, causing the diabetic to become unconscious.

When diabetes is first diagnosed, the doctor and dietician devise a basic diet that will perfectly balance the amount of carbohydrates consumed, and the amount of insulin available in the sufferer's blood. An individual diet is usually required for each person. The diet not only needs a given carbohydrate content, but also must suit the individual's normal eating pattern, and consider his food likes and dislikes. In the

Do you pick up the salt shaker before picking up your fork? Salting your food before tasting it may be an unconscious habit, and it's not a good one. Too much salt can aggravate kidney problems, and may also affect blood pressure.

early days of his illness, the diabetic must weigh everything that contains carbohydrate to make sure the correct carbohydrate balance is maintained. After a while, however, the diabetic usually becomes so knowledgeable about carbohydrate values that he can assess the carbohydrate content of a meal at a glance.

If you are cooking for a diabetic, it will be a great deal easier if he or she can eat most of the foods you cook for the family, and then make simple adjustments—by substituting fresh fruit for a sweet pudding, for example. You will need to make a few changes in your cooking methods, though. For example, you'll want to thicken gravies and sauces with beaten egg instead of cornstarch, arrowroot, or flour; substitute crushed starch-reduced rolls for bread crumbs; and follow the same rules for use of sugar recommended in the high cholesterol chart

High Sodium Foods

If your doctor has prescribed a low sodium diet, you will receive a detailed diet sheet. Here are some general guidelines, however, to help you plan family meals that avoid high sodium foods.

▶ All cheeses, except unsalted cottage cheese; salted butter, margarine, bacon fat. Any meat or fish that is smoked, cured, or pickled; canned, frozen, and bottled meat and fish products, including fish sticks, meat pastes, hamburgers, frankfurters, sausages of all kinds.
The natural sodium content of eggs, most other meat, fish, and poultry is fairly high.

▶ These foods contain sodium in a form other than sodium chloride : any product made with baking powder ; any food containing monosodium glutamate (MSG, the crystalline powder that enhances the flavor of food). It must be listed on the label if it is included in the product.
All dried, crystallized, or glazed fruits.

▶ All commercially prepared cakes, desserts, puddings; salted nuts, and peanut butter. Spicy crackers and crisp toasts; all breads and cakes unless especially made "salt-free"; most breakfast cereals, pasta, and rice cooked in salted water.
Canned vegetables; canned or bottled sauces, soups, and stocks, including stock cubes.

that you'll find illustrated on pages 106-107.

Most diabetics are advised to keep below average weight. For those who are too heavy when the disease is first diagnosed, a stringent reducing diet will be prescribed. The diet itself will be low in carbohydrate, and will help the person get used to the "carbohydrate values" and "carbohydrate exchanges" he will have to consider for the rest of his life.

If the diabetic does not have a weight problem, he is usually allowed the sugar substitute called *sorbitol*, which is a sweet white powder occurring naturally in some fruits. *But check with your doctor first.* Sorbitol is related to sugar. It is also a carbohydrate, and has a similar caloric value. The reason diabetics can use sorbitol is that it is only slowly absorbed from the digestive system. Unlike glucose, which enters the bloodstream quickly and raises the blood sugar level rapidly, sorbitol has little effect on the blood sugar level. It is not as sweet as sugar, and is widely used in special diabetic foods such as jams, chocolates, fruit drinks, and canned fruits. But beware of its caloric value. Sorbitol is better considered as a treat, and then only for diabetics who show no tendency to put on weight.

Saccharin is a much better bet as a sweetener, because it has no energy value at all. However, it is best to try to shift the diabetic's tastes gradually away from sweet foods in general. If he or she slowly loses the urge to eat sweet foods, the chances of succumbing to the temptation of eating something unsuitable—such as a cream puff or a candy bar—are lessened. Anyone who has ever tried a low carbohydrate diet knows how desirable the forbidden high calorie

Whether or not you're on a special diet, you should always have a nourishing breakfast in a relaxed, unrushed atmosphere. In fact, all your meals ought to be taken unhurriedly and calmly if you are to get the best out of your food to build good health.

Below: a diabetic must have proper medication, and must stick strictly to a restrictive diet. If he does, he not only can live a full life span, but he can also live an active and normal life in every way—and even his best friends needn't know of his ailment if he doesn't want them to.

sweet foods can become. So if you or one of the family need to keep of clear of cakes, cookies, and chocolates, it is much better to make a determined effort to persuade yourself, or Betty, or Jimmy, that you don't really like them after all. After a few months of brainwashing, you'll find that your tastes really and truly have changed, and you won't want as many—or any—sweets.

If there's a diabetic in the family, it is probably best for all of you to begin cutting down on sugar consumption. Everyone will benefit. The diabetic will not feel that he is being deprived, any family member with a weight problem will find it much easier to reduce, and the children will need far less dental treatment. Sugar is not a dietary essential.

There is no reason to restrict starchy foods for the family, however. The diabetic is usually allowed a certain daily allowance of these foods. If he keeps to his allowance, everyone else can eat as many starchy foods as they usually do.

Another important point to remember is that while most of us can skip a meal, or go for relatively long periods without food, the diabetic cannot. This is especially true if he is taking insulin. Soon after his customary mealtime has passed without his having eaten, the diabetic may have a feeling of shakiness, followed by faintness, and then unconsciousness. So when there's a diabetic in the house, meals should come for him regularly—every four hours, or whatever interval the doctor has advised. In special circumstances, you may need emergency supplies of food. For example, never set out on a long journey without taking a packed meal. Cars can break down miles away from a restaurant, and the diabetic will be in serious trouble without food.

Whatever your medical problem, you can live a more normal life by obeying doctor's orders, and carefully sticking to any prescribed diet. If you have a tendency to cheat on your diet occasionally, think about it first. Your life could be a little longer if you resist the temptation.

Left: children who de-
velop a strong sweet-
tooth as toddlers can
later develop diabetes as
adults. The diabetic's
inability to use carbo-
hydrates can be built up
over years of eating a
great many sweet foods.

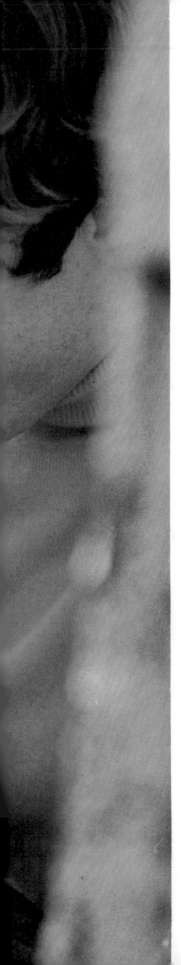

Feel Better-Look Better

7

Glowing health gives you glowing looks, whether you are a natural beauty or not. In fact, there can be no real beauty without an underpinning of good health. It is the sense of feeling well that makes you look your best.

If eating a well-balanced diet is a deeply ingrained habit with you—if you always have your daily quota of proteins, minerals, and vitamins, and enough, but not too many, calories—then you can be sure that you are making the best of the looks you were born with. Good food lays down the foundation of good health, and helps to keep the body well maintained throughout adult life. Because good food, good health, and good looks are so closely related, we can say that good food helps to give you the outward bloom of good health, and the inner radiance of vitality. The figure, skin, eyes, hair, teeth, and nails all act as mirrors of good health. We look most attractive when we are feeling really well. But we cannot expect food, however nourishing and well balanced, to work miracles.

It is largely a question of what genes you are born with that determine the type of bone structure, skin, hair, and teeth you have. It may or may not add up to our current opinion of beauty. But, remember, what we consider most beautiful and desirable today might not have ranked so high a few hundred years ago. Portraits of 18th-century European women claimed as great beauties show that many of them suffered from swelling in the neck, and the slightly protruding eyes symptomatic of goiter. Their condition was due to a dietary deficiency of iodine, common in many inland areas of Europe at the time. It is doubtful whether these beauties would be acclaimed today as they were in their own time.

Many women who are extremely attractive are not, strictly speaking, beautiful when you examine their features in detail. In

115

contrast, many beautiful women do not seem attractive. They seem to be lacking something—be it personality, vitality, or some indefinable magnetism.

Where does food fit into our concept of beauty, or physical attractiveness? Simply that food, as the basis of good health, is like a beauty aid: a properly balanced diet will keep you looking your own personal best.

On the other hand, if you pay no more than lip service to good nutrition, you are not making the best of your own good features. If you have been eating wrong for any length of time, it is inevitable that your health and looks will have suffered. Eating wrong means depriving your body of certain essential nutrients, or providing it with an overall surplus of food. Most bad diets are based on eating too many sweet foods, and too little protein, milk, fruit, and vegetables. The poor often cannot afford the kind of diet they should have. But, even among the better off, there are cases of malnutrition. It is not because of lack of food, but because of too much of the wrong kinds of food.

You may know exactly what you should eat, but find "forbidden fruits" so much nicer. Good nutrition is not only knowing what you need to eat, but also putting this knowledge into practice. It's rather like the golf enthusiast who buys book after book on golf. He knows exactly what he should do to improve his drive, but he just can't seem to do it on the green. People who have a bag of chocolates or peanuts nearby while they're watching television may not even give a thought to the fact that they could be ruining their health and looks. Some women —often those who are first-class cooks—can't

Even though there is no single type that can be called "the American beauty," there are some qualities that can be called typical of American beauty. These are wholesome good looks and energetic vitality, both of which are the rewards of eating healthfully. You are halfway on the road to looking good if you are in top health.

117

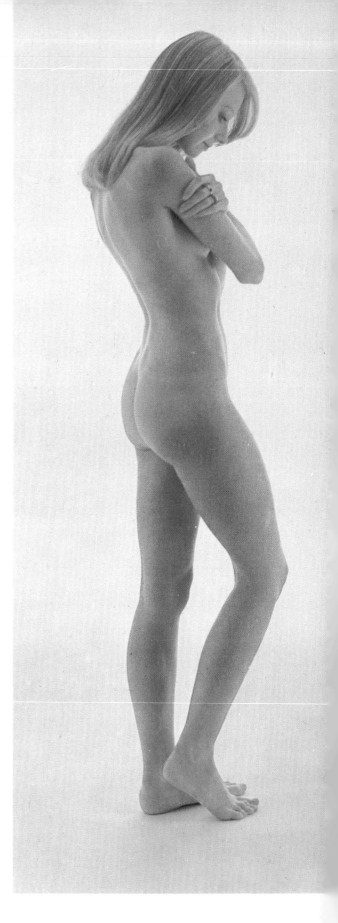

Your skin, hair, and nails depend largely on one ingredient: protein. Since protein cannot be stored in the body, you should eat at least 60 grams daily. For a dewy skin, your body needs vitamin A, found in liver, eggs, and leafy green vegetables, plus vitamin C daily.

seem to help nibbling cookies straight from the oven, or slices of homemade bread thickly spread with butter.

Compulsive eaters who turn to food when they're worried; hard-pressed executives who don't want to stop for a proper meal, and make do with a high calorie snack; house-wives alone at home who won't bother to cook or prepare lunch, and have a candy bar and a cup of coffee instead—these are only a small proportion of people who slip into bad eating habits. The long-term result can be that the individual is overfed-but-under-nourished. The body may be calling out for essential nutrients, but it is forced to accept excess calories in their place.

It is all too easy to fall into bad eating habits, and the habit of eating too much is, perhaps, the easiest bad habit of all. People overeat for a number of different reasons. It may be simply that they enjoy their food enormously, or it may be that they have a deep-seated psychological problem they are not fully aware of. Whatever the cause, overweight is the most common sign of poor eating habits. Look out for the giveaway signs, such as bulges around the tops of the thighs, an extra inch or so around the waist-line, zippers that strain, and buttons that pop. If you are surprised to find that you have put on a few extra pounds you didn't notice, take a grip of the situation now. Remember that one pound of surplus weight can lead too easily to another. So, if your weight begins to creep up, take stock of what you are eating.

Are you especially fond of sweet foods? Do you eat more of them than you know you should? If so, limit yourself to just one

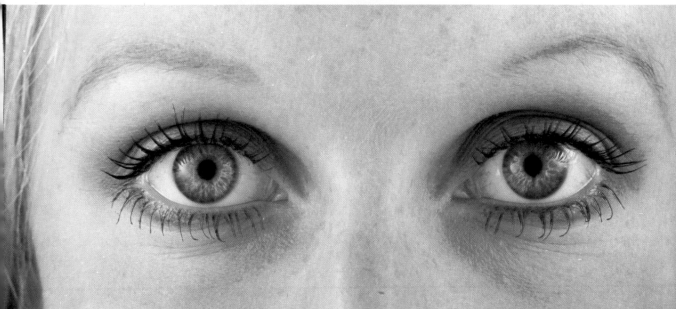

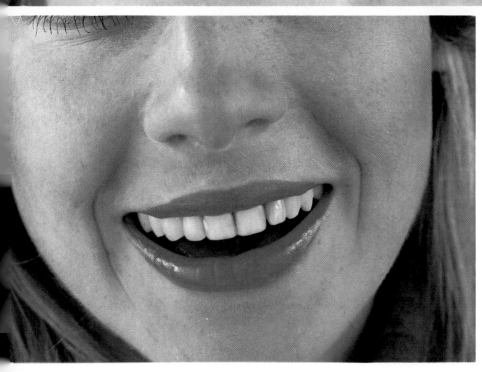

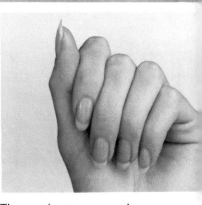

The nutrients you need for shining hair and strong nails are protein, calcium, and B complex vitamins. You get these in eggs, vegetable oils, liver, and brewer's yeast. Healthy teeth require calcium and vitamin D, which you can get in milk, tuna fish, butter, and enriched margarine.

Left: the simple lemon is a versatile beauty aid, known since ancient times as a boon to hair and skin. That's not all. A lemon hair rinse combats excessive oiliness, and fresh lemon is an active astringent for your face. A drink of lemon juice in hot water an hour before breakfast is great for your skin and eyes.

Right: your kitchen can provide some excellent beauty aids at a fraction of the cost of commercial products. Many preparations are based on the simple techniques of brewing or crushing herbs. Create your own cosmetics for an individual stamp of beauty.

sweet food a day. If you have dessert after dinner, have fresh fruit at lunch—and don't snack with the children after school. Do you find it impossible to throw away food that the children or your husband leave, or do you finish off all bits and pieces after meals? Steel yourself to tossing uneaten leftovers into the garbage can—unless there's enough for another proper meal, or you store the oddments in the refrigerator to eat as a snack when you need one. Don't do this with sweets, of course.

A poor skin can be a clear sign that you are eating wrong. Spots or blemishes may mean you are having too many sweet or starchy foods, and too little fresh fruit, vegetables, and salads. A pasty, lifeless skin can be due to constipation, which can usually be corrected by taking more roughage in the diet through wholegrain cereal foods, fresh fruit, and raw vegetables. The high content of vitamins C and A in fruit and vegetables are necessary for a healthy skin. Fresh air and exercise also help to improve the blood circulation, and bring sparkle to the complexion.

Unfortunately, you can eat a perfect diet, and have enough fresh air and exercise, but still not have the fine translucent skin that people often long for. Again, it's the luck of the genetic draw. If you have the right genes, and also eat the right diet, you will probably have the clear, smooth skin that we consider to be the most beautiful. Although beauty writers have been urging us for years to apply masks, lotions, and creams to our faces, none of these have any improving effect on the texture of the skin. Creams are an efficient

way of cleaning the skin, and oils help to lubricate the skin and prevent excessive dryness. But the actual texture of the skin depends on the thickness of the different layers that make up the outer body covering we describe as skin. The number of sebaceous glands that pour oil onto the surface of the skin to give it its natural lubrication, and the level and balance of sex hormones also determine what your skin will look like. These factors are all outside our control. We are simply born with them.

Another inherited trait is the thickness of the *collagen* in your skin. Whether you get wrinkles early or late in life depends on the type of collagen you have, how elastic it is, and how thick the layer. Generally speaking, the fine, thin skin that looks so wonderful early in life tends to wrinkle sooner than the

thicker type of skin. Perhaps this is nature's way of compensating us, so each of us has a chance of some beauty at certain times of life.

Many people think acne is caused by eating a diet with too many sweet, starchy, or oily foods. Although these foods may aggravate the condition, they are not the cause of pimply skin. Acne is found only among those with very oily skins. It is also most common among teenage boys, because the hormonal balance in the blood, especially the quantity of male hormones, determines the chance of having this skin problem, and the balance is unsettled during the teens.

In good health, the natural secretions of the sebaceous glands in the scalp coat the hair with a thin layer of oil so that the hair looks glossy and shiny. If you don't eat a

Dining in the comfortable, congenial setting of your own home, or at a pleasant restaurant, you and your favorite man can enjoy a warm closeness. The way to a man's heart may be through his stomach—if his dinner companion and the dining atmosphere are as appetizing as the food itself.

properly balanced diet, your hair can become what is most aptly described as lifeless. It loses its gloss, bounce, and depth of color. This color fading should not be confused with graying.

Graying cannot, unfortunately, be held at bay by good nutrition. Nevertheless, gray hair can look healthy and attractive. How soon you go gray, if you go gray at all, also depends on your genes. The tendency to baldness in men is also hereditary, except that premature baldness is found among severely malnourished individuals who have an acute shortage of certain vitamins.

In some instances, malnutrition—or simply the lack of good eating habits—can cause the fingernails to become thick or brittle, or to split easily, and break. But it is difficult to relate any single condition to a

shortage of any single nutrient. Contrary to widespread belief, gelatin, which is a rather poor source of protein, can have little or no effect on strengthening the nails. Conditions of the nails are often affected by psychological stress. Unhappiness and worry seem to make the nails weak, or easily broken. The same psychological factors tend to upset people's dietary habits, so their diet may be implicated in some indirect way. It is impossible to pinpoint any way that a particular change in diet can improve the nails; however, if you don't eat properly, your nails could become worse.

Before we were born, the food our mothers ate determined how strong our teeth would grow. Calcium and phosphorus, and vitamins A and D, are needed to build the material of which the teeth are made.

Obviously diet cannot determine whether teeth are straight, and diet cannot change yellowish teeth into naturally white ones. However, an important effect diet can have on teeth is in relation to decay and disorders of the gums. If you eat too many sweets, the teeth are left with a coating of sugar, and the bacteria normally present in the mouth break the sugar down into acids, which attack the enamel of the teeth.

Fruits, salads, and vegetables clean the teeth almost like a toothbrush by removing the surface coating of sugar left after eating something sweet. They also scour out any sticky pieces that may be caught between the teeth. Crisp, hard foods also help to keep the gums healthy. The modern tendency is to eat highly refined, soft textured foods. These don't need much chewing, but they can

easily fill up the spaces between the teeth, and encourage gum-infecting bacteria to grow.

Gingivitis is the most common gum infection found in adults. More severe infections can affect the teeth themselves so badly that they may all have to be extracted. A simple precaution is to include crisp, hard foods such as fruit, vegetables, salads, crusty breads, and nuts in the diet. Regular brushing, and twice-a-year dental checkups can insure dental health.

Looking around some of the most exclusive cosmetic counters today, you will find that many of the high priced preparations sound rather like gourmet foods. Many cosmetics and beauty aids proudly claim to contain eggs, milk, avocados, cucumber, lemons, strawberries, or other natural ingredients such as essential oils and herbs. This seems to be part of the "back-to-nature" cult that is very popular in the mid-70's.

Centuries ago, before cosmetic scientists were allowed vast sums to spend on research to find new beauty aids, women had little to help them in the quest for beauty. Washing the skin with milk is a treatment dating from those long past days. Cleopatra went to the extreme of taking a daily bath in ass's milk. Oriental spices were used to perfume the body. A mash of strawberries was found to remove freckles, then considered as blemishes. Now that we believe a sprinkle of freckles enhances good looks, we can eat the strawberries instead.

Perhaps a more beneficial method of using many food components in cosmetics would be to eat them. Remember, we cannot absorb more than minute quantities of

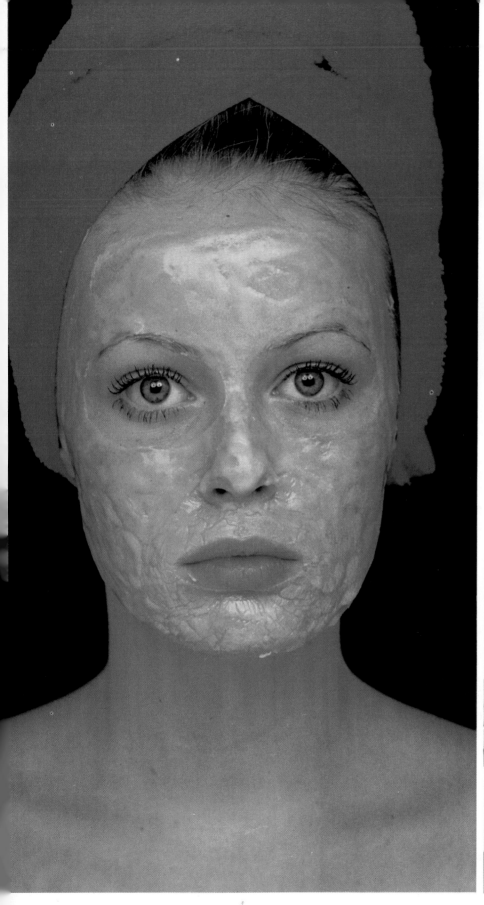

Above : whipped egg whites applied around the eyes with cotton pads is a temporary remedy for crow's feet. Leave the whites on just until they begin to draw slightly, and wipe with astringent. Below : moistened rose hip tea bags help to reduce undereye puffiness.

substance through the skin. Experiments have shown that even the most highly emulsified ingredients are absorbed only slightly. In prepared cosmetics, the oils are whipped to a froth so that each oil droplet is minute, and stand a better chance of being absorbed through the skin than an oil that is simply smeared across it.

Many beauty aids these days are made with basic nutrients such as amino acids (the protein constituents), lipoproteins (proteins combined with naturally occurring fats), essential oils, and vitamins. Some products also contain female sex hormones that are thought to arrest the normal changes occurring in the skin as a result of the unavoidable aging process. Again, these constituents are absorbed in only minute quantities, which many scientists consider ineffective to carry out the claims often made for the product.

Some of the beautifying properties of certain products that have been used for many years are still being put to good use. Old-fashioned lanolin, the oil derived from sheep's wool, is the basis of many beauty creams. Lemon juice and other slightly acid products have an astringent effect, which helps to remove certain oily secretions from the skin. Eggs contain the lipoproteins that are incorporated in many hair products. These lipoproteins improve the appearance and manageability of the hair because they reduce its natural static electricity. There is no reason why you should not use the egg itself in place of a commercial hair rinse. Take care, though, when washing out the beaten egg you apply to your hair after shampooing; if you use water that is too hot, you end up with a head of hair mixed with scrambled egg.

Some women still rely on oatmeal face masks to clear the skin; witch hazel to brighten the eyes; lemon to lighten the hair; and vinegar rinses to remove any dulling film after washing the hair.

Psychology plays an important part in the beauty business. If you feel well and happy, you usually look good, too. If you feel a little low, bored, or depressed, the chances are your looks will reflect the way you feel. Most people know how depressing it is to be told that they are looking tired or unwell. The opposite also holds true. Confidence plays its part. If, for example, you think a diet is helping you to reduce quickly, and have every faith that you are going to be able to lose all the excess weight you want to, the chances are you will stick to the diet. If someone else recommends a diet to you, but you don't think it will help you lose weight, the chances are that it won't. If you are sure that anything is going to do you good, whether it is a health food, vitamin pill, or an avocado face mask, you're halfway there to feeling or looking better.

For centuries, we have known how a good meal served in pleasant surroundings makes one feel more relaxed, refreshed, and at peace with the world. Generations of women have taken advantage of the mellowing and comforting effects that a beautifully prepared and delicious meal has on men. Whatever you might hear to the contrary, the contribution of food to romance is psychological. No special food has that mysterious stimulating effect that many people give it credit for. Even oysters won't make you amorous if you eat them while having a row with your husband.

The giving and receiving of food symbolizes part of the deep-seated psychological origins of love. This starts with maternal love in the early days of life, when a mother feeds her baby. Many of our attitudes to food, life, and love are formed when we are children. They are all closely tied in with family mealtimes, with the offering and rejecting of food, and with withholding children's privileges associated with food. Young lovers who like to share a meal on an evening out, and settled couples that enjoy a celebration meal in the comfort of their own homes—both are reenacting the display of love symbolized by food.

Eve was tempted by the juicy apple for very good reasons. Crisp apples clean the teeth better than any toothbrush will—and apples help keep gums pink and healthy, and the mouth beautifully fresh.

Questions & Answers

More is known about nutrition today than ever before, but it is still a comparatively new science. In fact, although masses of material are published on the subject, it's not always easy for the average person to get clear, uncontradictory information when they need it. This applies not only to day-to-day meal planning, but also to special situations, such as when your child has been prescribed a gluten-free diet against a celiac condition, or your grandmother slips into malnutrition simply because she can't adjust her diet to allow for an inability to chew well any longer. With Americans spending some $60 million or so a year on vitamin supplements, it is clear that we feel our diets are inadequate, and we don't know how to improve them by food alone.

These questions and answers will help you add to your store of nutritional knowledge, and, at the same time, clarify some of the food myths that abound today. Would you like to know what to do when your sick child refuses all food? How can you help an elderly father reduce his bouts with indigestion and flatulence? Do the claims for vitamin E as a kind of "fountain of eternal youth" have you galloping to the drugstore for these expensive vitamin supplements? Are you trying to decide whether you should take pills as a way of losing weight? In the following pages, you will find practical guidance on such questions as these.

Also given are some welcome ideas about planning a dinner party so that each course complements the other for an overall balance of taste and texture, and some suggestions for vegetarian dishes in case you have to serve someone who doesn't eat meat. Other helpful information includes: a discussion of yogurt and sea salt as health aids; tips on cutting the food budget through better shopping; an explanation of what wholegrain is, and how some wholegrain substitutes can be made for the usual rice and cereal; and details about diabetic sweeteners and diets. In all, this section will set you further on the path to making your daily food the *Food for Life, Love, and Looks.*

Eating out of doors has a special delight all its own, and there's a health bonus, too. The fresh fruits and raw vegetables that are so easy to pack and eat are also good for you.

Diets for the Sick and Old

In these days of miracle drugs and advanced medicine, I'm surprised that my doctor put so much emphasis on a special diet for my sick son. Can you explain this?

The explanation is simple. With or without wonder drugs, diet is an essential part of the cure of many illnesses—and the major part in the treatment and cure of some. It all starts, of course, with the fact that a sound diet is the basis of good health. It stands to reason, therefore, that modifications in what you eat daily can be used to give your body more or less of certain foods you need to return to, or maintain, good health.

Not knowing what illness your son has, I might just point out some uses of diet in treating the sick. Diet is the only known cure for a celiac condition, in which food cannot be absorbed properly. This illness usually strikes infants and young children, but can occur at any age. Diet is also important in treating hepatitis, and in controlling many of the diseases of the kidney. You must already be familiar with the emphasis on diet for those who have diabetes, heart conditions, and ulcers.

If your family does not insist on fried and fatty foods, on rich sauces and desserts, or on a great many sugar carbohydrates, you can often manage to fit the preparation of the special diet into preparation of family meals without much extra to-do. If the family does insist on a rich and heavy diet, perhaps it's time for a modification for the whole family.

There is a case of a celiac condition among my relatives, and I would like to know something about the diet in preparation for a coming visit of the sufferer.

Fortunately, it is relatively easy to conform to the special diet for a celiac condition, which simply must be free of gluten. This means eliminating anything made with wheat, rye, oats, or barley. Although the list of foods to be avoided seems long, the foods that are allowed can easily be part of the general family diet. It is better not to do special cooking for the person with a celiac condition, especially if a child, so that he or she can feel normal in eating with others.

The most important diet control is gluten-free bread, which may have to be baked at home if not available in the stores. Also on the banned list are macaroni, spaghetti and other pasta, sausages, canned meats and fish, stock cubes, cheese spreads, mayonnaise, wheat and oat cereals, peanut butter, cocoa, and ice cream—in fact, most canned and packaged commercial goods.

My husband's busy executive life has finally hit his stomach, and he has a bad case of peptic ulcers. He's having almost nothing but milk right now, but is supposed to go on a low residue diet in a few weeks. Can you give me some details about such a diet? The doctor simply gave me a mimeographed sheet

with a couple of paragraphs about it.
One of the most important things to know about any treatment for ulcers is that the sufferer must eat often, if sparingly, of easily digested foods. This will help absorb stomach acid, and keep the acid from touching the sore spot (ulcer), which causes great pain.

The low residue diet is also called a low fiber, low roughage, bland, or gastric diet. The point of it is to avoid food having coarse fibers, because they can irritate the stomach and intestine. Coarse-fibered foods include most raw fruits; wholegrain cereals; nuts; dried beans and peas; stringy vegetables, such as celery and green beans; stringy fish, such as lobster and crab; and stringy meat, such as some steaks. Also to be avoided are foods of strong taste or flavor, such as onions, radishes, pickled herring, strong coffee, alcohol, salt, pepper, and any highly seasoned or spiced dishes.

Since worry and stress are often at the root of the ulcer victim's problems, it is helpful if the family can make mealtime calm and pleasant. Eat slowly, avoid arguments, and don't fuss over the dieter. If he simply doesn't want to eat, let him have a warm milk drink, and offer a light meal after he's had a rest. Generally, be guided by what he would like to eat as long as there are not too many starchy foods.

Now, what can your husband eat? The meats he's allowed are probably also liked by the rest of the family, so should be served often: roast or broiled chicken, turkey, lamb cutlets, or boiled ham. His vegetables must be mashed or sieved—but you can do his portion after cooking them for the family meal: potatoes, carrots, young peas, spinach, asparagus tips, cauliflower. In the fruit line he can have baked apple, pared peaches, apricots, or pears; ripe bananas; ripe melon; and most juices. For dessert: custard, jello, ice cream, applesauce, sherbert, mild yogurt, vanilla pudding, or pound cake.

Is there anything harder than getting a sick child to eat properly? I'd be grateful for some tips on this problem.

Children not only lose their appetites easily when sick, but they also tend to be extremely fussy, even turning down things they usually like. We know how important it is for them to eat right, both to regain strength and to continue normal growth. Here are some things to try to coax a sick child to eat:

1. Make a nice color mixture—such as yellow carrots and white potatoes as vegetables, and red jello as dessert—and serve the food on pretty plates.

2. Serve small portions of everything, and individual cups of custard or pudding; allow second helpings.

3. Use drinking straws. Milk in a tall decorated glass with a little flavoring or coloring will appeal more.

4. If your child doesn't like eggs on their own, use them in puddings, add them to mashed potatoes, or make a soufflé or other supper dish in which they are the main ingredient.

5. If your child is a slow eater, use an insulated plate to keep the food warm for as long as she is eating.

6. Don't let your child see you are worried if she doesn't eat; help feed her if necessary, but don't keep it up too long.

My daughter loses weight and looks wasted when she gets tonsillitis or a bad cold. How can diet help?
Diet is important in treating all illnesses of which a fever is a part. This includes influenza, tonsillitis, measles, chickenpox, bronchitis, and pneumonia, among others. The weight loss is aggravated by the loss of protein from the body, which results from a fever. The diet must restore the lost protein, and help to build up the body's resistance.

As always in treating sick children, several small meals are better than three big ones. Check with your doctor before you use any diet modifications, however.

In the early stages of treatment, you'll want to concentrate on giving the child primarily milk foods: milk itself, cream soups, ice cream, milk shakes, rice or arrowroot puddings, custard. When the appetite begins to return, add lamb cutlets, chicken, ground beef, cooked egg dishes, chopped vegetables, and fresh fruit. Liver is excellent if the child will eat it. Bread and cereal may also be added in the second stage, but only if the child will eat it in addition to, and not instead of, other foods.

My elderly father, who is living with me, is robust and has a good appetite. However, he has been having indigestion and flatulence more often lately. Is there something we can do in the way of diet to help him?

It should be an easy matter to avoid attacks of indigestion or flatulence in a healthy elderly person, such as your father. But, you must remember at the start that, with increased age, the ability to digest food decreases. Slight modification in the diet is, therefore, necessary.

Although older people usually like strongly spiced food because of their diminished sense of taste, strong spices can contribute to indigestion. They should, therefore, be avoided as much as possible. Other strongly flavored, strong tasting foods that may cause indigestion in the elderly, and should be crossed off the list, are ripe cheese, pickled fish or vegetables, and vinegary sauces.

Fatty meats, such as pork, duck, and goose, and rich creamy sauces are not easily digestible, and this also goes for fried food in batter. It will be easier to avoid indigestion, too, if pastry and sweets are cut down in general, especially between meals.

Strong vegetables are a common cause of flatulence, so your father shouldn't eat cabbage, Brussels sprouts, cauliflower, dried peas or beans (including baked beans), and raw onion, for example. If he loves onions, try boiling them so he can then enjoy their flavor without their possible side effects.

The doctor told my grandmother the reason she has trouble with digestion is that she doesn't chew her food enough, but she can't chew well because of her dentures. What is she supposed to do?

If the cause of your grandmother's indigestion is swallowing chunks of food, she can easily solve the problem of not chewing well by adjusting the consistency of foods. For example, she doesn't have to give up roast chicken if she likes it, but she should take the meat from the bones and chop it before eating. Grinding beef or lamb means she could keep these two meats on her menu. Serving them with sauce or gravy moistens them nicely, and adds flavor, too.

Cheese is an excellent and inexpensive substitute for meat, so encourage your grandmother to eat it regularly. To avoid swallowing lumps or pieces, which can lead to indigestion, she can grate it, use it in a main dish, or melt it in soups or sauces. If she gets tired of, or doesn't like, soft boiled eggs, let her mash hard boiled eggs, and add mayonnaise or other dressing.

Fresh fruits and lightly cooked vegetables can be mashed, chopped, or put through a sieve. Bananas don't need this treatment, of course. Custard, jello, light puddings, and ice cream are easy to eat as well as being well liked. Many stewed fruits are soft enough to eat without further treatment. Pureed vegetables, or vegetables in casserole dishes or soup, also soften enough for her to eat easily.

I always thought that a diabetic just had to cut sugar out of his diet, but my husband, who has recently been diagnosed as diabetic, is restricted to eating only unsaturated fats. Is this a common thing?

All diabetics must restrict their intake of sugar, and their diets are designed with this in mind. However, there are variations in diabetic diets, and the unsaturated fat restriction is a more recent one.

The diabetic who is on a sugar free diet has to cut out all sugar. This is the simplest of the diabetic diets, but it is limited to those having a very mild case of the disease.

The unsaturated fat diet has become more important in the treatment of diabetes in recent years, although there is still a great difference of opinion about it among doctors. If your husband is on a strict altered fat diet, he will probably have to eat 80 per cent unsaturated fats regularly. This is a difficult diet for Americans, who partake heavily of saturated animal fats in meats. But, if it is essential to your husband's well-being, you must all work to help him adjust to it.

Among the changes that will probably have to be made are replacing butter with polyunsaturated margarine, and replacing whole milk with skimmed; using polyunsaturated vegetable oil or margarine in cooking; limiting egg consumption; cutting out cream; cutting down on fried foods; and cutting off all fat from meat.

Remember, a diet prescription is a very individual thing, and the one your husband has been given has been carefully worked out for him. So, in helping to care for him, discourage him from temptations to try a simpler or easier diet.

You say that diabetic diets are an individual thing. Are there other kinds besides the ones already mentioned?
Yes, there are at least three other diets that may be prescribed for diabetics.

The *limited fat* diet is usually given to diabetics who are also overweight. In this diet, the total amount of fat allowed is extremely low. Often the whole daily allowance will be used up just in meat.

In *exchange* diets, choices can be made among various foods within the same class of proteins, carbohydrates, or fats, and a given number of meat, milk, fruit, vegetable, and bread exchanges are allowed. Thus, a person might have some salad dressing or light cream for the fat exchange; eggs or chicken for the meat exchange; crackers or potatoes for the carbohydrate exchange; and orange juice or raisins for the fruit exchange. This is an easy diet to apply once it is understood, but it takes a thorough and careful explanation. The other diabetic diets can be worked as an exchange diet, and most are.

The *weighed* diet is for the gravest cases of diabetes. It is exacting and complicated, requiring the use of scales that weigh by grams. It must be remembered that grams of protein, carbohydrate, or fat does not mean grams of *food*. Therefore, if six grams of fat are allowed, this means an amount of food that yields six grams of fat—even if the food weighs more or less than six grams. Diabetics need a good set of food value tables as well as an accurate scale.

What are the sweetening agents that diabetics can use instead of sugar, and how do I substitute one for sugar in recipes?
To answer the last part of the question first, you had better follow the manufacturer's instructions in substituting another sweetener for sugar in cooking or baking.

As for the substitute sweeteners diabetics can use, they are mainly as follows:

Saccharin. Sweeter than sugar itself, this compound has no caloric value at all. It is the oldest of the sugar substitutes in use. Some who use it complain it has a bitter aftertaste. Saccharin should not be used if a food is going to be cooked or frozen after it has been added, because the taste changes and the sweetness decreases. It is best when added just before serving, as in coffee or tea.

Sorbitol. This compound is a carbohydrate, and has caloric value. This means it can be fattening, and that it must be counted in the daily calorie allowance. However, because sorbitol doesn't affect the blood sugar level very much, it is often allowed in moderation for diabetics. Sorbitol is the sweetener most commonly used in dietetic candy, gum, and jam.

Lactose. This is also a carbohydrate requiring that its calories be counted. It is only moderately sweet, and, therefore, is sometimes combined with saccharin.

You should find out from your doctor which, if any, of the substitutes he feels is all right in the case under treatment. If he doesn't specify one, you may have to test various ones to see which is most satisfactory in taste to the diabetic.

Vitamins and Health Foods

If I had a glass of orange juice for breakfast every morning, would I need more vitamin C that day?

Yes, you would still need somewhat more. A few ounces of orange or grapefruit juice at breakfast will go a good part of the way to fulfilling your daily requirement for vitamin C, which is about 60 mg., but not all the way.

An average juice glass of frozen orange juice, which is the most widely used form in the United States, will supply about 40 mg. of vitamin C per glass. Freshly squeezed orange juice yields about 48 mg. in three ounces. This leaves between 12 and 20 mg. of vitamin C to make up the rest of the day. Of course, you can get the additional amount from leafy green vegetables, berries in season, or other fresh fruit or fruit juices.

Remember, the body cannot store vitamin C, so you must be sure you get enough each day. You needn't worry that you'll get too much, either, because the body gets rid of what it doesn't need.

Vitamin A is supposed to improve your eyesight, and also to increase sexual response. Is this true?

A *shortage* of vitamin A can have adverse effects on eyesight and sexual response, it is true. But it does not follow that more vitamin A will improve either, if you are already getting the proper amount of it.

There have been cases of office workers who have increased their need for vitamin A because they work under florescent lights, and use their eyes continuously. Their need showed up not only in the degree of eyestrain, but also in skin blemishes.

Simultaneously with visual difficulties and skin problems, a diet deficient in vitamin A causes abnormalities in the mucous membranes of the body. These are the delicate linings of the tracts of the digestive, respiratory, urinary, and reproductive systems. A lack of vitamin A may cause the membranes of the reproductive system to dry out and harden, so reducing an individual's sexual responsiveness. With sufficient intake of vitamin A, you will help keep the mucous membranes lubricated, as they should be.

There is little reason for anyone to be short of vitamin A, because the recommended requirement of 5000 units per day can be met with a single serving of carrots, yellow squash, green beans, broccoli, apricots, or spinach. We also store vitamin A in the body. Experiments to try to induce a deficiency of this vitamin have taken years when the subject was well nourished.

If we were to believe all we read, everyone would be taking vitamin E like mad for a great sex life. Can you tell me the truth about the effect of vitamin E on sexual potency?

There is a great deal written about vitamin E, a well-known but little understood vitamin. It has been referred to as the "fertility vitamin" since 1920, when it was noted that rats could not breed without this vitamin in their diet. Subsequent tests on human beings have led to no clear scientific conclusions about the vitamin's effect on sexual potency. However, when the results of animal experiments were publicized, the public linked vitamin E to sexual benefits for humans.

The chemical name for vitamin E is tocopherol, meaning "child bearing." This tends to encourage its reputation for being a miracle antisterility medicine. There are some studies which have shown that after taking vitamin E, mothers with a history of miscarriages or premature births bore healthy infants. There have also been experiments in which fathers who took vitamin E several months prior to conception showed an increase in the number and quality of sperm. Vitamin E, then, seems to have some effect in the treatment of habitual miscarriage, and, perhaps, in preventing the birth of defective children. There is no assurance that the vitamin will change sexual potency in those who use it only for that purpose.

I have heard that sea salt tastes better than regular salt, and that it is also better for health. Is this true?
Most people who use it would certainly say that sea salt tastes much better than ordinary salt—and, in fact, has a pleasant taste if you try a pinch on its own. Because of this added flavor, it is used more sparingly than table salt of the usual variety.

There are several factors that make some nutritionists say sea salt is healthier than regular salt. One of these is that sea salt contains other salts, and, in particular, iodine, in addition to the sodium chloride of which common salt is composed. It is already well known that iodine is necessary to good health. Eating sea salt, therefore, can supply a daily quota of iodine.

Even if you are not on a low sodium diet, you should not take excessive amounts of sodium, according to some nutrition experts. You use less salt in general if you use sea salt, so this is one control on intake of sodium.

One problem about using sea salt: it is not available in big supply. Only a small amount is produced for retail sale because of the difficulty in finding uncontaminated sea areas, and of evaporating what salt is found under natural conditions. If you can't get sea salt, you should always use iodized salt to make sure you won't go short of iodine in your diet. Most stores in the USA stock iodized salt.

What does the term "wholegrain" mean? Is wholegrain bread better for you than white bread, as most health food enthusiasts say?
In wholegrain flours, the entire grain kernel—that is, the bran, starchy endosperm, and germ—are all part of the flour. Even after the milling and sifting processes, the rich flavor and high food value of the original seed is reserved. Wholegrains can be wheat, corn, rye, buckwheat, millet, rice, oats, or barley, and all these grains can be milled as flour. They can also be used in their hulled form, or in meal form.

There is a difference between wheatmeal, or brown, flour and bread, and whole wheat, or wholemeal, products. Just because you see the word wheatmeal on a brown loaf of bread, don't think you are getting *whole wheat*. You aren't. Wheatmeal and brown are terms applied to any flour that falls between white and whole wheat. It can describe a bread in which the flour has 72 to 99 per cent of the wheat grain. You should insist on whole wheat or wholemeal bread if you want to get one that contains the bran and the wheat germ. Baking your own bread has its obvious advantages: besides knowing what is in it, you can vary the grain make-up.

Health food enthusiasts, supported by many nutritionists, point out that the bran content in whole wheat bread provides roughage needed by our body, which white bread does not. The wheat germ of wholegrain bread also contributes vitamins A, E, and B complex, plus protein, to the diet. Another consideration for those who want to—or must—watch their weight, is that wholemeal bread is approximately six calories less per ounce than white bread.

What are some of the other cereal grains I can use as a change from rice and noodles?

There are numerous varieties of cereal grains, and you might find that the family takes to one or the other at first taste. Brown rice, either in short or long grains, is unpolished rice that retains much of the bran layers. It is more nutritious than white rice, and has a more pronounced flavor, but it takes longer to cook. Freshly hulled millet is a pale yellow grain that can be combined in casserole dishes, or used as the main ingredient in a soufflé. It can also be used as a hot breakfast cereal, or, in flake form, as a cold one. Millet has a sweetness of flavor that makes it go well as a pudding dessert, and is also a good meat extender.

Buckwheat, or kasha, has been the staple of the Soviet diet for generations. Mixed with meat, sour cream, mushrooms, and chicken livers, kasha can be a sophisticated dinner party dish. It can also be eaten with milk for breakfast, with vegetables for lunch, or on its own as a side dish.

Wild rice is a native American grain—and not a rice at all. It grows wild in the shallow lakes of Northern Minnesota. Because its harvesting is a slow, complicated one, the cost is high. However, wild rice can be used in small quantities in combination with other grains for added flavor.

For a change in the kind of noodles you use, try the green spinach ones you can get in Italian speciality stores. They come in many of the pasta varieties you'll want: spaghetti and lasagne, for example.

Some of my friends who are on a diet have mentioned yogurt as an important diet food, and many magazines and newspapers print recipes with yogurt these days. What exactly is yogurt?

Yogurt is an edible sour milk product that is highly digestible and nutritious. It looks a little like sour cream, and is in fact made in a similar way. The distinctive, sharp taste of natural yogurt comes from the special bacteria *Lactobacillus bulgaricus*, which control the souring process. These bacteria grow and multiply in milk, breaking down the milk sugars into lactic acid. Yogurt gets its smooth texture from the way the lactic acid acts on milk proteins.

Most commercial yogurt is made from skimmed milk, so it is low in fat. Because it is also rich in protein and calcium, and often has vitamins A and D added, yogurt is often recommended to dieters. Compared to 165 calories in one cup of whole milk, plain yogurt made with skimmed milk has 120 calories in one cup. Fruit and flavored yogurts have sugar added, and, therefore, are much higher in calories. For nutritional value, yogurt is equal to the quantity of milk from which it was made. Fruit yogurt, of course, also has the nutritional value of the added fruit. On the whole, yogurt can be a pleasant alternative to milk.

I have been convinced that yogurt is good for me—and I even like it—but is there any truth in the claims that yogurt cures all kinds of ills, and lengthens life?

Although yogurt is acknowledged as being remarkably healthy, it has no proven medicinal value. Neither is there scientific proof that yogurt contributes to longevity. The basis of this claim lay in studies of the long lived peasants of the Soviet Republic of Georgia, and villagers in the Himalayas. However, it cannot be said without doubt that their longevity comes from eating yogurt, any more than from a generally healthy way of life.

Modern interest in yogurt was started by Dr. Ilya Metchnikoff, a Soviet scientist who isolated some unique bacteria from the Bulgarian drink *yahourth*, which is essentially the same as our own yogurt. He believed that the long lives and good health of the Bulgarians could be attributed to the bacteria in their national food. Yogurt, however, is not a new food. It was known to the Biblical peoples of the Middle East.

136

Diets for Losing Weight

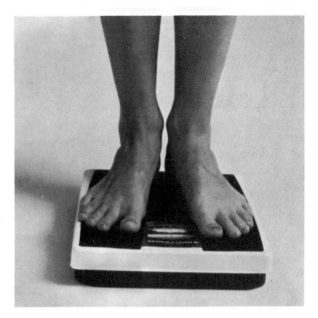

There are so many reducing diets printed or recommended by friends, how can I be sure which is right for me without trying a succession of them?
First of all, you should always consult a doctor before going on any diet at all. For, you must bear in mind that what is good for your friend or the neighbor next door is not necessarily the best for you. The high protein diet that your husband is happy on may be unsuitable for you. You may feel more comfortable, and lose weight more painlessly, on a "little less of everything" kind of plan. In any case, you can go a long way toward making a good decision on a particular diet—even when prescribed—by analyzing yourself and the life you lead.

For example, you may be put off—and your digestion may suffer from—a low carbohydrate diet, which is high in fats, and generally, rich. Others don't mind cutting out the bland fillers, mostly carbohydrates, and can eat and enjoy such a rich diet. You must ask yourself if you can afford the expensive meat, fish, and other foods on a high protein diet before you choose this route to weight control.

Do you have time to cook separately for yourself, or do you try to fit your diet into normal family meals? If the latter, it might be better to simply try to restrict your carbohydrate intake. Do you hate to count and add up calories that may go as high as 1500? Perhaps you won't mind counting carbohydrate grams, which only go to 60.

Should you increase or decrease the amount of water you drink when you're on a diet?

Unless you have a special medical reason why you should cut down on your intake of water, you should always drink plenty of water—on or off a diet. Water acts as the body's conveyor belt, helping in the vital filtering action of the kidney, and in the elimination of waste substances. Too little water slows down this essential process, and begins to dehydrate the body.

Many people find the six to eight glasses of water recommended on some diets is too much for them, but even the more moderate recommendation to dieters is to drink four to six glasses daily.

Although you shouldn't restrict the amount of pure water you drink, you do have to watch your intake of drinks that have an energy value of their own. Alcohol in any form is usually out. Milk and fruit juices are allowed in limited amounts. Coffee and tea are unlimited, if you keep to your daily milk allowance and don't add sugar. Low calorie soft drinks can be drunk in moderation.

My sister-in-law went on a crash diet about three months ago, and lost about 15 pounds. She also lost her appetite, and now finds it difficult to eat more than a tiny snack a few times a day. Her husband cannot convince her to see a doctor. Could she become seriously ill?

137

She could certainly become seriously ill, and, from the symptoms you describe, she may be ill already. It is entirely possible that she is suffering from a nervous lack of appetite caused by severe, unsupervised dieting. This condition often results in such a distaste for food that eating becomes almost impossible. The general medical opinion is that this problem occurs more frequently in women than in men, and most of all in girls who have just gone through puberty.

Lack of appetite and inability to eat are both a pathological and psychological state, and can only be cured by medical care. It often requires psychiatric help. Whether she wishes to or not, your sister-in-law must be persuaded, or if need be, frightened, into seeing her doctor. Like everyone else, she simply cannot survive without nourishment, and it sounds as though she is not eating nearly enough to obtain adequate nourishment. Convince her that the longer she waits to see a doctor, the greater harm she is doing herself. It might help to show her articles describing the terrible effects of this condition on women. Even if her problem is not as serious as the medical condition mentioned, her nutrition imbalance is serious, and should be given prompt medical attention.

Am I wrong to want pills to help me stay on a diet? Are such pills harmful to children?

It would be much better for you if you could manage to stick to your diet without drugs, and, in any case, you should use them only for a short period of time.

Some dieting pills may be dangerous in some cases, so they should be prescribed by a doctor familiar with your particular dieting problem. Some pills, such as methyl cellulose ones, are not actually drugs. This substance swells up inside your body, giving you a feeling of fullness, and helping to stop the most acute hunger pains. There is usually no reason why children can't take methyl cellulose pills, but be sure to check this with your doctor before your child does so.

Don't expect overnight miracles from pills, either. Reducing aids are designed to act as a crutch to help you get started on a diet. They are meant to be used over short periods of time, and should never be taken for much longer than it takes to lose the first few pounds. There are some pills that can be taken over a three- to five-month period, but even this is long. Let your doctor be your guide.

Never give appetite reducing drugs to children. It is far better for overweight children to learn to control their food intake, and to modify their eating habits for a lifetime pattern.

I lost weight slowly but steadily on my diet for about three months, and was delighted about it. Now, however, I haven't lost an ounce for about two weeks, and discouragement is setting in again. What can I do about this?

This kind of thing happens frequently. It seems that you can go along losing weight successfully for three months or so, and then come to a dead stop, still short of the weight level you wanted to reach. There's nothing to worry about, though, if you're still sticking honestly to your diet.

What probably has happened is that your body has reached a plateau, and is adjusting to its new weight before getting rid of more fat. It's a kind of stabilization, and, the longer you can stabilize your weight at this lower level—even if it's not as low as you'd like yet—the longer you are likely to keep from regaining weight.

There's something else that should be extremely encouraging to you at this time. You should find that, even if the scales don't show a loss of weight, your body measurements should show a loss of inches. Try on a dress that was too tight before, and see how much better it fits. Take a look in the mirror, and notice how much flatter your abdomen looks. Your waist certainly must look smaller, too, and your bust.

So, keep to your diet now that you're well on the way to reaching your goal. You'll soon find that you start losing weight again.

Some General Questions

Should everyone have three regular meals a day for proper nutrition? Can't I get what I need in two well-balanced meals, which I prefer to three?

Most nutritionists recommend three well-balanced meals a day as a general rule. This pattern of eating reduces between-meal hunger to a minimum, and better suits energy requirements throughout the day by being less of a strain on the nervous and digestive systems. Often, a breakfast of some protein, fruit, and small amounts of fat and starchy carbohydrates (the latter preferably of the wholegrain variety) will keep you from feeling starved and weak by lunchtime. Moreover, for dieters, it will help prevent overeating at lunch, and make a diet easier to stick to.

Perhaps some individuals can work out two well-balanced meals a day, and stay in peak health on such an eating schedule. But, unless you know your nutritional needs exactly, it's wiser to take the advice of the experts and have three meals each day.

I have uncontrollable cravings for sugar. Sometimes, in fact, I have eaten a whole box of candy by myself. Is it possible to be addicted to sweets?

Many nutritionists would say that it is certainly possible to be addicted to sweets. One recent authority on dieting, Professor John Yudkin, has gotten wide publicity on his views about the harmfulness of sugar. He believes that there are people tempted to eat excessive amounts of sugar carbohydrates because their bodies have grown to require them. His conclusions are based on discoveries of the tremendous changes that take place

in the functioning of the body when sweet foods are consumed in big quantities.

Sugar consumption, he claims, alters the chemistry and hormonal action of the body in an alarming way. People who consume large amounts of sugar reduce the ability of the body to cope with its own blood sugar, making them slightly diabetic. Sometimes the uric acid in the blood increases toward the high levels associated with gout.

That's not all. Studies have shown that the structure of the liver and kidney is changed by excessive sugar intake, and that two powerful hormones are increased. These physical changes prod the brain to crave sugar, just as an alcoholic or drug addict craves drink or narcotics.

The cure for the so-called sugar addict is the same as for other addicts: total withdrawal. Sugar must be cut out of the diet completely. If not, there is always the danger of taking "just one" chocolate or cooky, and starting the bad old habit again. It may take six months or so for a heavy sugar user to break away from sweets. When cured, however, he or she will more than likely be a slimmer and healthier person.

I would like to add a bit of variety to my meatless menus that call for cheese, but my family dislikes Swiss and Provolone,

and I seem to be stuck with American and Cheddar. Can you suggest other cheeses I might try?

If your family is not fond of Swiss, try using Gruyere or Edam together with the Swiss in a soufflé or pasta dish—and use natural rather than processed as much as possible. Many processed cheeses become rubbery when they are melted.

Mozzarella, the pizza cheese, is an excellent melting cheese, not only for tomato dishes, but also for egg and meat dishes. Muenster is one of the best melting cheeses, and can be used on its own, or combined with other cheeses. Longhorn and New York State are types of Cheddars. Try them for a change from your usual Cheddar.

Gouda, Edam, and the American versions of spiced Gouda and smoked cheese make delicious appetizers, served hot and bubbly. Italian ricotta cheese is becoming more popular in this country. It is akin to cottage cheese, but creamier and smoother. It is surprisingly good in an omelet, and is a must for lasagne. Liederkranz and brick are two American-born cheeses, Liederkranz being a less strong version of the German Schlosskaese.

Even though I try to eat a balanced diet, my skin is always broken out. I seem to have more blemishes than when I was a teenager. Is there a special diet that would improve my complexion?

It is a recognized fact that a diet high in protein and rich in vitamins, followed over a long period, will contribute to a healthy skin. However, the key word always is balance. A very high protein diet may contain too many fats for your particular system. So, get a balance of fresh green vegetables, fruit, and wholemeal bread or cereal into your daily intake of food. Vitamins A and D also contribute to a good complexion. That means you should have liver, eggs, citrus fruits, and milk regularly.

You might also try to cut out fried foods, rich desserts, pastry, chocolate, and anything high in fat or sugar. Some people find that starting the day with fresh lemon juice, taken with hot water, aids their complexion. Plenty of water, and fresh green vegetables lightly cooked, plus salads, may also show results. In working toward a nicer skin, don't expect an overnight change. Allow your system at least 28 days to adjust. If you stick to an improved diet at least this long, you will probably see a change for the better.

Why is it necessary to add color to some foods?

There is no necessity at all for artificial food coloring. Consumer expectation of what a food should look like is the reason manufacturers give for the use of color additives. Take the example of canned peas. Pale green peas, slightly varied in size, are not as popular as the bright green large ones.

The loss of their color in canned green vegetables is due to the high heat necessary for sterilization. Heat processing may also have some effect on canned fruits—you probably have had canned strawberries of a brownish color. So, because some foods lose much of their color during the canning process, the so-called natural color is put back in.

We consumers must take much of the blame for the unnecessary coloring agents added to foods. For example, one food firm tried offering sausages, canned peas, and cakes with no added color. The result: they were left on the shelves.

I try buying less expensive cuts of meat, such as short ribs, spareribs, and pork loin chops, but somehow they don't seem to go as far, and I'm not sure I save any money. Can you clarify for me whether the bony less expensive cuts are, in fact, cheaper than meaty more expensive ones?

The most important thing to remember is that it's not the price per pound, but the price *per serving* that counts. You can only decide if you are saving money on meat by figuring out the cost per serving.

As a guideline, a serving is usually defined

as three ounces of cooked lean meat. However, keep in mind that two ounces comes closer to a serving for young children and older people, and a larger portion is necessary for teenagers. Meat with a substantial amount of fat and bone, such as rib chops, brisket, spareribs, short ribs, and T-bone and porterhouse steaks, yield only one to two servings per pound. Roasts, poultry, ham, and certain chops give two to three servings per pound. This means that, many times, the meat you pay more for per pound is cheaper because it gives more servings.

Your best buys are the boneless meats—stew meat, ground meat, flank and round steak, liver, kidneys, and other variety meats. If you learn to use the tender, but meaty, cuts in slowly cooked stews, flavored with herbs and fresh vegetables, you'll be providing your family with meals that are economical as well as nutritious. Another buying tip: large roasts, ham, and poultry are not as popular in the summer months, so they are priced lower for the wise shopper.

Fresh mushrooms are always so expensive. Would I be more economical if I used canned ones only?
You might be surprised to learn that canned mushrooms are more expensive than fresh ones. Even the less desirable and cheaper stems and pieces cost 50 per cent more than whole fresh mushrooms. The way to save on mushrooms is to buy in quantity when you find the price is a few cents lower. You can freeze them if you own a deep freeze, or you can sauté them lightly, and then store them in the freezing compartment of your refrigerator. Mushrooms freeze and keep well.

It seems a waste of time, energy, and gasoline to shop in two or more supermarkets for the best prices. Am I wrong on this?
Comparison shopping is the only way to find out price differences among food stores. In trying to make your food dollar stretch these days, it is to your advantage to get the best price you can on everything that goes into your food basket. Of course, driving five miles to save 25 cents on groceries is pointless. But, even in the suburbs, at least one or two different stores are generally close to each other, and you should compare their prices.

Scan the newspapers and supermarket handouts for bargains in all stores in your area. It may mean that you have to spread your shopping over two or three days, perhaps for three-quarters of an hour each. Don't forget that the European housewife shops nearly every day, not just because her refrigerator is small, but also because she can adjust her menu to take advantage of what's cheaper and more plentiful each day. It is better not to make a practice of purchasing foods that are uncommon to your area, because they will always be expensive. Save such foods for special occasions.

I have a good general idea about planning well-rounded meals for the family, but I'd like to have a quick, easy, and reliable reference that I can use to make sure our diet is as healthy as possible. What do you recommend?
The U.S. Department of Agriculture publishes a Daily Food Guide, which specifies the amounts of certain foods you should eat daily from each of four main food groups. It is handy, easy to follow, and gives some equivalents so that, for example, you know you can serve two eggs in place of two to three ounces of any meat, poultry, or fish.

Here is the way the Daily Food Guide demonstrates what you should aim for in the daily family diet:
Milk Group:
2 to 3 cups for children under 9 years
3 or more cups for children 9-12 years
4 cups or more for teenagers
2 cups or more for adults
3 cups or more for pregnant women
4 cups or more for nursing mothers
Meat group:
2 or more servings daily
Count as one serving:
2 to 3 ounces cooked lean beef, veal, pork, lamb, poultry (off the bone), fish; 2 eggs;

1 cup cooked dry beans, peas, or lentils;
4 tablespoons peanut butter
Vegetable and fruit group:
Count as one serving $\frac{1}{2}$ cup of cooked vegetable or soft fruit, or one piece of fruit.
Include daily:
One serving citrus fruit or other good source of vitamin C
2 or more other servings, including potatoes
Include every other day:
1 serving dark green, yellow, or orange vegetable for vitamin A
Bread-cereals group:
4 or more servings daily of wholegrain or enriched products
Count as one serving:
1 slice of bread
1 ounce of ready-to-eat cereal
$\frac{1}{2}$ to $\frac{3}{4}$ cup cooked rice, pasta, corn meal, grits
Using this guide, you can easily plan menus for a week or two, and do your food shopping accordingly.

Our supermarket often has bruised fruit and wilted salad greens and vegetables at greatly reduced prices. Is it smart to save money by buying them?
It is the opposite of smart to buy fruits and vegetables that are not fresh—and the more bruised or wilted they are, the worse it is. Vitamin C loss starts from the moment these foods are harvested, so if they are well past their peak by the time you buy them, they will probably have none of their vitamin C left. The golden rule of fruit and vegetable buying is: the fresher the better.

My family is not too fond of fish, and, to make matters worse, I can never think of what to serve with it. I'd like to have it once in a while, so can you give me some suggestions of good go-togethers?
Most fish is delicate in taste, so you should serve vegetables that will enhance, rather than overpower, its flavor.
The following suggestions go deliciously with fish, and will also add a bright dash of color to the whiteness of the main dish: peas, string beans, broccoli, spinach, asparagus, chicory, corn, mushrooms, peppers, eggplant, tomatoes, squash, zucchini, or carrots.

Green or mixed salads, too, go well with fish. Remember to use French dressing if the fish has been cooked in a sauce, poached, or steamed, and a mayonnaise or thousand island dressing if it's been fried or broiled. Cole slaw is another excellent accompaniment for fish.

If your family counts potatoes a must, do them boiled, mashed, or creamed with poached, steamed, or sauced fish. With fried or broiled fish, try French fried, hash brown, or baked potatoes.

Large fish are especially tasty if you stuff and bake them. Shrimp and crab make a very rich stuffing, but a simple bread stuffing often adds the best touch.

I can easily plan the main course and vegetables for dinner parties, but I get bogged down on what goes with what for appetizer and dessert. Once, when I was practicing sauces, I had a rich sauce with every course—and it was too much of a good thing. I'd like to have some tips on meal planning for dinner guests, please.
You're on the right track to start your planning by settling the main course in detail. Then, think of the meal as a whole.

Each course must have its own special interest, which it will not have if there is a repetition in tastes and flavors. For example, don't start with chicken soup if chicken pilaf is your main course, no matter how delicious each is. If you're having a robust main course, such as steak or roast pork, stay away from meat paté for the curtain raiser. Is lobster the feature of the meal? No shrimp cocktail for the first course, then.

Besides considering likeness of taste, you must also think of lightness and heaviness of texture. If the main course is a heavy and filling one, keep the appetizer light. Is it lasagne or spaghetti as the main course?

Start with a light soup, such as consommé, half a grapefruit, or melon. Alternatively, if you've chosen a light main course, serve a hearty soup, such as minestrone, a cheese soufflé, or a scalloped seafood dish to start.

Apply the same set of rules in choosing the dessert. Has the meal up to then been generally light? Then, go to town if your specialty is baking, and have a fruit pie or chocolate cake. If the meal has been on the heavy or rich side, have a dessert of fruit laced with liqueur, a custard, or sherbet.

One last check to make in your mind. Imagine the whole meal on the table. Will it be colorful enough? Do you need a garnish to brighten up one of the courses? Will Melba toast make a nice touch—and crunch—with the first course? How about a light cooky or wafer with dessert? Think ahead like this, and you're bound to have a beautiful dinner that your guests—and you—will enjoy.

My 15-year-old son, who eats like a horse, has just decided he's a vegetarian. I hope it's simply a passing phase—he gets these sudden enthusiasms—but, meantime, what on earth can I feed him besides macaroni and cheese?

Many delicious and nutritious vegetarian main dishes are made from beans of various kinds, because beans are a good source of protein. In fact, when we think of the Mexican staple of rice and beans as two starches, we are making a mistake. The combination of rice and beans creates a complete protein, whereas beans on their own are an incomplete protein. So combinations of vegetable proteins is something to keep in mind in providing your son with hearty, filling, and healthy meals.

Some of the main dishes that come quickly to mind:

Try a lentil and vegetable stew. This combines lentils with potatoes, zucchini, onions, celery, seasonings, and spices, the lentils cooked alone first for a couple of hours, and the rest added and cooked until done. Bay leaf is a good spice for this, but you can use any other favorite. Add chopped parsley, crushed garlic, and lemon juice for the last few minutes of cooking.

Did your son like chili con carne in his meat eating days? Give him a kidney bean casserole that resembles it, but has no meat. Soak dried red kidney beans overnight, drain, and cook for about 1½ hours. Drain again. Add fried onion and garlic, chopped tomatoes, and a teaspoon of chili powder, salt, and parsley. Put in a greased casserole, decorate with sliced tomatoes, and sprinkle a little wheat germ over the top. Bake in a hot oven for 10 minutes.

Bring out some of your favorite Lenten egg main dishes, too, and don't forget things such as pancakes, rice casseroles, thick soups with hearty wholemeal bread, spaghetti and other pasta with meatless sauce, peanut butter sandwiches, and nut cutlets. It's advisable to get a good vegetarian cookbook, of which there are many new ones these days.

When it's muggy and hot during the summer, I just can't face cooking or eating. (I am a widow, living alone.) My daughter tells me I should force myself to eat. Should I?

You probably already know that the answer is "yes, you should eat." The real question is how to make it an attractive idea when the hot weather puts you off.

The first thing you might consider is to have five or six small snack meals during the day, rather than three big meals. (With a little planning, this can be done even if you work rather than stay at home.) If you include plenty of cheese, cold creamed soups, tuna or salmon salads, and eggs, you'll get most of the proteins and vitamins you'll need. For the nutrients you need from vegetables, try cooking them lightly first, chilling them, and eating them as a salad with a mayonnaise or lightly seasoned French dressing.

You can see from these suggestions that much cooking is not necessary. If cold food appeals to you when it's hot outside, that's what you can have—as long as you still keep a balance in your diet.

143

For Your Bookshelf

Living Nutrition
by Frederick J. Stare and Margaret McWilliams, John Wiley & Sons, Inc. (New York: 1973)

Contemporary Meal Management
by Mary Kramer and Margaret Spader, John Wiley & Sons, Inc. (New York: 1972)

Let's Cook It Right
by Adelle Davis, Harcourt, Brace Jovanich, Inc. (New York: 1971); George Allen and Unwin Ltd. (London: 1971)

How to Shop for Food
by Jean Rainey, Barnes & Noble Books (New York: 1972)

Feed Your Face
by Dian Dincin Buchman, Doubleday & Co. Inc. (New York: 1973); Gerald Duckworth & Co. Ltd. (London: 1973)

The Live Longer Cookbook
Cooking With Natural Foods by Leonard Levinson, Bantam Books, Inc. (New York: 1973)

Diet and Heart Disease
American Heart Association, 44 East 23rd Street, New York, N.Y. 10010

Food: Readings from Scientific American
Introductions by Johan E. Hoff and Jules Janick, W. H. Freeman & Co. Inc. (New York: 1973)

Picture Credits